THE
PEOPLE
SPARK ®

A Business Leader's Essential Guide to Crafting Your Culture With Confidence

Erin Mies
Kristen Ireland

KH PUBLISHERS

The People Spark®: A Business Leader's Essential Guide to Crafting Your Culture With Confidence

Published by KH Publishers.

Printed in the United States of America.

Print ISBN: 978-1-953237-11-8
E-Book ISBN: 978-1-953237-30-9

Cover & Interior design by Dez Carter, Designs by Dez

The People Spark® is dedicated to the agribusiness leaders that lead every day with your hardworking commitment, from before sunrise to well after sunset. We see you and we appreciate all of the things you do (that many may not even notice) to make sure that your business is making the difference and impact on your families, your businesses, and your communities.

TABLE OF CONTENTS

THE

PEOPLE
SPARK®

FOREWORD

"Everyone has a plan until they get punched in the mouth."

– _Mike Tyson_

S eems a little strange to start a book about building a company culture with a quote like this, doesn't it? As we thought about all the things we wanted to be sure to capture and address in this book, this really resonated with us about the realities of being a leader, a business owner, and a human in general.

In our work with agribusiness clients each day, we make plans, we assess the punches, and we coach them through to stay focused on the goals at hand. The plans aren't the outcome, though. The business results and the culture they've created are.

In writing The People Spark®, we wanted to provide our readers with the same framework we use with clients in our consulting business, encompassing both how to build the goals, strategies, and plans to get the business results you want, and equipping you with some of the tools we help clients develop so you're building the culture you actually want!

There is so much that leaders can do to impact the culture within their teams and their organizations that it can feel overwhelming, and tough to know what to do first. We're business owners ourselves

- we GET it! This book is intended to break down the most critical areas within your business that can have the biggest impact on your culture. Think of it as the 80/20 Pareto Principle for culture.

You might be surprised that while we're "technically" HR consultants, this book doesn't preach to you about how to complete onboarding forms the right way, or the in's and out's of performance reviews. Why? That isn't our focus with our clients, and it isn't our focus for you.

Our goal is to drive behavior change – to ensure that the behaviors you want to see in your business are the behaviors you actually are seeing! Surprisingly enough, filling out a performance review doesn't make that happen (I know, the cat's out of the bag now!).

As you work through this book, we encourage you to go section by section, and take time to reflect, think, process, and act on what you read. How does it apply to your business? How do you know that your employees know what to do? How do you know you're successful?

It's our pleasure to share this with you.

INTRODUCTION

W e are so glad you're here. The fact that you picked up this book, thumbed through it, and even read some bits of it already tells us that you are invested in your business, its success and the key role your team plays in that success. Or it says that you're on the lookout for some magic that will help inspire your team's culture and improve your business.

While I'd love to say we're magicians, the truth is that we're not. Nor do we have a silver bullet that will "fix" any cultural problems you might be dealing with today. Everything we will cover here is about the simple things that will significantly impact your business and your culture when done *consistently*.

We are going to get into the details. Promise. Before we get there, let's step back and talk about why this is important in the first place. Our businesses succeed, and we succeed, because of our employees. Your most valuable resource is your employees. It's corny and cliche, and you've heard it before. And yet it is so true. Think about your rock star employees—the ones who bring it every day and go above and beyond their call of duty. THEY are the ones that will make your business successful!

Evidence supports the positive impact those rock star employees (engaged employees) have on your business. According to the State of the American Workplace published by Gallup in 2017 when comparing business units in the bottom quartile of engagement, those in the top quartile realized improvement in these areas:

- 41% lower absenteeism
- 24% lower turnover
- 28% less shrink (depending on the industry, also known as scrap)
- 70% fewer employee safety incidents
- 17% higher productivity
- 21% increased profitability.

I have yet to meet a business owner or leader who WOULDN'T want to see those numbers. I know that as a business owner, I would! Who would say no to lower absenteeism, lower turnover, fewer safety incidents, AND higher productivity and profitability?!?

So, yes, we all want it, but how do we get it?

Here's another study by authors Marcus Buckingham and Ashley Goodall in their book, *Nine Lies About Work: A Freethinking Leader's Guide to the Real World*. Buckingham and Goodall built on Gallup and Korn Ferry's studies to determine the critical factors for engagement. In studying engagement surveys and engagement results, Buckingham and Goodall found that eight factors were disproportionality present in highly engaged teams:

- I am enthusiastic about the mission of my company.
- I am surrounded by people who share my values.
- My teammates have my back.
- I am confident in my company's future.
- I clearly understand what is expected of me.
- I get to use my strengths every day at work.
- I know I will be recognized for my excellent work.
- In my job, I am challenged to grow.

Notice there are two broad categories within these eight factors.

One type focuses on the business and team, referred to by Buckingham and Goodall as the "WE experiences." The other category focuses on the individual or the "ME experiences."

As we proceed through this book, we will focus on our end destination—business growth and business success. How we get there is through engaged employees, including finding, hiring, and retaining engaged employees. Every section and chapter will provide information on the practical, simple and intentional steps you can use and implement as a leader to reach this destination. Every section and every chapter are another step in that direction.

ABOUT US

Before we get too far, we should tell you more about us. We have a lot of passion and experience in human resources, and we're self-proclaimed "HR Geeks." We wear it as a badge of honor. We have more than forty years of experience in varying human resources roles. Our passion shows us in our geekiness. We know it, own it, and take it as a compliment when someone tells us.

We believe in the businesses with which we work. We believe companies will be successful when their employees are engaged and *pulling* in the same direction. We know that by intentionally defining and aligning your culture, goals, and HR practices, you, your business, and your employees will all be successful. We've seen it work, too. It is possible for you and your business.

We founded People Spark® Consulting because of our passion for helping small and mid-sized businesses rethink their human resources processes and practices. Our goal is to pull them out of the rut of feeling like they "have to" or "should" implement procedures because it is "best practice." We strive to introduce confidence, effectiveness, and harmony in those we serve. Our ultimate objective is to eliminate wasted time, energy, and resources on activities that don't positively impact business results or employee engagement.

Here's something else you should know about us. We don't like process for the sake of process. We often hear other HR people talk about the need to implement or roll out a new form as part of their approach to making improvements. Pretty soon, everything feels like a process, form, or checklist. When this happens, we see entire teams just going through the motions, checking the boxes, and wondering why they aren't achieving the desired results.

Now, don't get us wrong. We understand that processes are essential, and forms are necessary. But procedures and documents are not the end game—they are simply a mechanism used as part of achieving the ultimate business goals. We will talk about processes and forms. And we will discuss them in terms of their direct relationship to the business's goals, culture, mindset, and skill set of leaders to achieve the goal, and the leaders' ability to reach the destination of business success through engaged employees.

PLAY TO WIN

A couple of years ago, my family vacationed on the beaches of North Carolina with two other families. We were blessed with great weather, our kids' first trip to the ocean, and great friendships. My husband and I also had the opportunity to learn a few new card games, including a new favorite - Shanghai Rummy.

My family didn't play cards growing up. I vaguely remember learning how to play *War* with my cousins while playing at my Grandpa's house when we were little, but that's about it. As a young adult, I'd attend the occasional euchre tournament and had to be re-taught how to play…Every. Single. Time. It just didn't stick. But Shanghai Rummy? Now, this game stuck with me!

Here's the deal: By the end of this ridiculous game, you are holding at least nineteen cards in your human fingers, trying to come up with two runs and two books with a bunch of other rules that others will tell you about only after you've committed violations. If you don't develop a case of carpal tunnel syndrome after playing this, you've already won.

The first night we learned, I played tentatively. As long as I didn't come in dead last, I thought, I would be happy. In the last round of that game, I laid down my cards (thinking I *actually* had something decent) and quickly heard, "What are you doing?! You could do so many other things with that card!" as the response from the others. I finished up the game sheepishly, and while I didn't finish in dead last, I didn't feel any better than if I had.

On my morning walk the following day, I dissected the previous night's game, and it struck me: I had been playing NOT TO LOSE so much that I didn't even put in the effort to try and WIN. *Are you even kidding me?!* I thought to myself. The athlete in me (it's been a few years, but that girl is still there), the competitor in me, couldn't even believe it.

When I returned to the house, a few other adults were up, and we started talking. And I unleashed the competitor. I shared with them that I realized that I had been trying so *hard not to lose* the night before, to play by the rules and not make a mistake and that they had better be ready for me to come out *prepared to WIN the next night*. The difference in my tone, confidence, and perception of my ability completely changed. I may not have won the whole game (there are ten rounds - I *told* you it was ridiculous!), but I won one enjoyably.

I reflected later upon this, and some parallels to HR in small businesses came through for me. The most glaring? As we work with more and more businesses, we hear about the "have-to-do" and compliance aspects of HR. And if we're being honest, those are the things that we must do not to lose. But how many of us *really* know what we can do to lead people and align HR so that our businesses can WIN? We often hear about the time commitment it requires, about not knowing *what* to do, or that there isn't a person in the organization that can lead it.

We have learned something else while working with small and

mid-size businesses. In many cases, human resources are seen as a necessary evil. It's the compliance focus, the CYA (cover your a$$), what you need to protect yourself and ensure that you follow all appropriate laws and rules, so you don't get sued or charged. Yes, compliance is an integral part of human resources. That said, looking at human resources *solely* from compliance or CYA perspective is a limited view, and it's playing NOT to lose.

The truth is, the WHAT to do and the HOW to do it isn't complicated at its heart. It takes attention, intention, and clear goals. If we are only playing NOT to lose, our businesses will never get their game face on to WIN.

Playing NOT to lose is:

- Focusing on human resources mostly as compliance.
- Implementing human resources processes without a clear tie to goals or objectives.
- Not defining your culture or values, or only defining your values because you feel you have to for the sake of your customers or investors.
- Believing that you are paying employees to do a job, and in return, they should do their job.

Many businesses may increase the focus on human resources, understanding that it can add value to the company, and businesses start to move further on the continuum. And start doing things like:

- Identifying resources or best practices (either from past employers or Google searches) to build processes.
- Implementing processes like interviewing, on boarding, and performance reviews.
- Communicating more with employees on expectations.
- Hiring someone (either full or part-time) to focus on human resources activities.

When a human resources team member is hired, anything related to human resources is placed on that person. They (alone, in some cases) are responsible for finding and keeping employees, addressing performance issues, ensuring employees are doing their jobs and staying around, resolving problems, and developing employees. While leaders are relieved to have someone dedicated to human resources responsibilities, they are still not achieving their goals. They are still playing NOT to lose rather than playing to win. It's not about WHO does the work, it's about how those individuals VIEW the work.

And some businesses unleash the power of their human resources, understanding their businesses are successful when their employees are successful. These businesses start:

- Intentionally defining the culture, values, and behaviors.
- Living and modeling these behaviors, even during the most challenging times, and making tough decisions.
- Incorporating these values and behaviors into their human resources practices so that everything is aligned to that intentional culture.
- Holding employees accountable for living the values and behaviors (and, even more importantly, ensuring that managers and leaders do the same).
- Proactively attracting high-quality candidates through strong culture and marketing to differentiate themselves as an employer of choice.
- Building trusting relationships with employees from the point of offer and incorporating values and behaviors into the success of the employee in the on boarding process and plans.
- Actively engaging employees by sharing business goals and success and aligning employees' work with the business

goals and strategies.

- Consistently making expectations clear and providing feedback through recognition, consistent coaching, and constructive feedback.

Leveraging human resources in this way is playing to WIN!

These are the things we will focus on throughout the book. Let's play to WIN!

SECTION

SPARK YOUR CULTURE AND GOALS

CHAPTER 1:

WHAT IS CULTURE?

Culture isn't what you say, it's what you allow.
-Fredrik Backman ("Beartown")

Culture. There are many buzzwords in business, and especially in human resources. Buzzwords can have significant meaning but are used so frequently and broadly that they start to lose their impact and meaning. **Engagement** is a buzzword (important yet overused in vast contexts). Another buzzword is **culture**, which is unfortunate because it is so powerful.

Have you ever heard the quote "culture eats strategy for breakfast" by Peter Drucker? As the quote indicates, you can have the best strategies, goals, and business plans— and none of that matters if you don't have the right culture.

Yet where do businesses tend to spend their time and energy? Strategies and goals. When a business isn't getting the results it wants or isn't achieving its goals, we often see the focus go back to changing the strategy or adjusting the goals. *Chances are, the issue is not the lack of strategy or goals; it's an issue of culture.*

Yes, we get it, we understand the need for a strong culture. But what the heck do we do to influence it? Culture seems so broad, so nebulous, so fluffy. Our aim here is to make it more specific so that you can take action on it.

Every organization has a culture, just like every family, religious organization, sports team, and club has its own culture. It's a "you can just feel it [the culture]" type of thing for many, making it so tough to describe. Since it comes across as so vague and ambiguous, it doesn't lend itself to be the topic that business owners want to talk about all that often. For some, it doesn't feel like they have the right words or enough information to do anything meaningful with it.

One facility I worked in was notorious for having consistently low engagement survey scores every year. Not just a little low, but the caboose of the entire organization. However, one thing we had in our facility was an identifiable culture. It may not have been the one we wanted, or our employees necessarily preferred, but we had one.

In one of our first strategy sessions around culture, one of my team leaders challenged me on our ability to change the culture. In his mind, the plant was the way it was, and nothing was going to change it. He saw culture as immovable or stationary. He and I discussed his perspective, and I shared that we needed to think about our culture as the outcome, not as the thing to influence. If we start with culture as the outcome, we can begin to see and become more aware of the behaviors and nuances that define what it is today. Those behaviors and nuances? They are far more pliable and in our scope of control than the big, fluffy culture concept.

Now, years later, working with our clients, we see organizations start to shift from an immovable mindset to one where culture can be influenced every day.

When we dug into culture further, we found the dictionary-specific definition to be "A set of behaviors or beliefs characteristic of a group." YES, exactly!

We mentioned earlier that every business has a culture that is felt within its environment. Think of the businesses you like to visit. Chances are, you enjoy visiting them based on how you feel while there. You have those positive feelings about the business because of the *behaviors* you see and the feelings you experience when you are there. Maybe it's that the employees know you by name, and they ask you how they can help or anticipate your needs before you ask.

We worked with a client a few years ago and visited one of their retail locations. While meeting the employees, a customer walked through the door and up to the counter. One of the employees greeted the customer by name and said, "I saw you drive up, so I grabbed what you needed, and I have it ready to load into your car." The customer didn't have to ask. The employee knew him well enough to know what he needed, anticipated it, and delivered it. There were several examples like this that we witnessed that day.

You may be thinking, "yes, that's great customer service." Seeing it in action, it was more than that. The action this employee took was more than just great customer service. This business has a culture of service, and it's not just a value they have listed on a wall or something they say in their advertisements. The employees were consistently behaving in ways that demonstrate service to customers.

Now think of the businesses you may not like to visit. You have a feeling, but it's not the feeling of wanting to go. It's the feeling of dread. Your feelings are based on the behaviors you see and the words you hear. In all of this, you are experiencing their culture.

Suppose you want to know the culture of a business or an organization. Watch the behaviors of the managers and employees. Your company has a culture. What is it? Stop and look around, really notice the behaviors of your employees. What do you see? What do you hear?

Many businesses espouse a culture full of wonderful words like teamwork, integrity, and innovation. They say things like we have "a great team environment," we are "fun," or we "innovate."

Please know what you say may not always reflect the actual culture. That's why it's necessary to look at the behaviors. Do you say we have a culture built on teamwork, yet team members make statements like "that's not my job"? Do you say we have an innovative culture, yet when changes are recommended, team members reply with, "we've always done it this way," or "that's not the way I was taught."

I was recently in a gas station with a sign that read, "NOW HIRING. Work in a team environment with fun team members." I walked in, and the employees were stone-faced. No one smiled at me, acknowledged me, and the employees didn't engage with one another. So much for their team environment with fun team members. When the stated culture and the actual culture are misaligned, it looks, sounds, and feels like this gas station.

Culture exists all around us, every day. It shows up in the littlest things, not just the big moments. Culture is defined by what we choose to stop and address [or not] with our staff or colleagues. When we make a choice and decide *not* to have a coaching discussion with a team member because we're "uncomfortable" and "don't feel like we have the right words to say," we are defining and refining our culture in those moments. When we allow behaviors from employees because "it's just how he is" or, "but she's really good with customers," we are defining and refining our culture in those statements. When we step into discomfort and ask the questions that need to be asked, even if it isn't perfect, we positively define and refine our culture. We define and refine our culture in the everyday, seemingly minor moments.

Reflect on this for a moment. How are you defining and refining YOUR culture every day? What are you choosing to act upon every day? What are you choosing to walk past every day?

CHAPTER 2:

BUILD YOUR INTENTIONAL CULTURE

Great, you might be thinking, *talking about culture and its importance is fine and good, but I have no idea where to start.* The good news is that it doesn't matter if you have zero employees or one hundred. You can always start from where you are. As C.S. Lewis said, "You can't go back and change the beginning, but you can start where you are and change the ending."

Think about your business and how you want to be known. We don't mean just with your customers and their interactions with you (these are important, too!). Go further: What reputation do you want as an employer in your community? Does your organization have values, defined or implied? What are they?

It can be hard to think about culture only in terms of behaviors. If you have a sense of the culture you want to create, there can be so many different behaviors you could focus on that it can feel overwhelming. We like to look at a steppingstone between culture and behaviors, with the first stone being your values. Defining these intentionally sets your People Spark® in motion.

- Values are the principles and standards you expect in your business.
- Values are the collection of related behaviors that point to aspiration in your business.

You may have defined your values and you reflect on them regularly as a business. Maybe they are posted on the wall, listed on your website for your customers to see, or included in the annual report for your Board. You may not have thought about your values at all. You know conceptually what is important to you and the feeling you want your employees and customers to have, but you have yet to define them.

We work with clients in both cases and will start where you are now.

STARTING PLACE #1:
YOUR VALUES ARE DEFINED

You have values defined and maybe a description of each value. You have an idea of how this value looks in your business. Take a moment to celebrate what you have done! This is great, and you can build from here. Here are the next steps:

If someone is demonstrating this value, what are the *specific* behaviors you are seeing?

Working with clients, we have found that if the behaviors are not explicitly identified, each leader and employee has their own idea of what behaviors demonstrate value. Talk to your leadership team or managers.

- Ask what behaviors they think demonstrate the value. Get specific!
- How have they seen employees demonstrate the values through their behaviors or not?

You may hear things like "that's not how I understood it" or "this is what it means to me." These statements are signals that the expected behaviors are not specific enough, and not everyone is on the same page.

Even more importantly, it means employees are getting different messages from their leaders, each heading in another direction. They may be doing what they THINK is right, but it's not what you have identified-for the business. A value of showing integrity may look like simply telling the truth to one team member, and it may extend beyond that with another team member, where it also means speaking up if something isn't right.

Here's another way to think about it: What employee behaviors drive you nuts when you see it happening in your business? Are there any behaviors you want to see demonstrated by your employees that are not included in any of the values you have identified?

This is also a time to reflect on whether or not the values that have been identified are *actually* what you want to see. Ask yourself and your leaders:

- What behaviors have the most significant <u>positive</u> impact on the business? Are they included or reflected in your values? Are there behaviors that your employees demonstrate that positively impact your business; that aren't yet included or reflected in your values?
- What behaviors drive you crazy? What behaviors make you cringe? How are these addressed in your values?

We see this frequently. We were working with one client to define their values – they had been focusing on values like community, respect, and integrity. After lengthy discussions, we heard a theme emerging and other CEO's concerns. He was frustrated. Frustrated because employees would only do the tasks in their job description and respond to others with "that's not my job." He was frustrated that they had just built a new building-the perfect setting for their clients. But employees were moving chairs and tables, bumping into walls, making holes, and didn't seem to care.

The thing that REALLY drove him crazy? The paper towel dispenser.

The dispenser had a way of tearing off a tiny corner that would fall to the floor, and employees would choose to walk right by, leaving it on the floor. He would walk into a brand-new bathroom with small pieces of paper towels lying all over the floor. Notice the theme? To him, this action of not picking up the pieces of paper towels on the floor demonstrated to him that the employees were not committed –to the clients, to each other, the environment, or to the business's success. As a result, we added a fourth value: Commitment. You can guess what type of behaviors were listed for that value.

Another client in a retail store had a different pet peeve. When customers would leave and say 'thank you,' employees would respond with 'no problem.' For him, hearing this sounded like nails on a chalkboard. In his mind, customers were *honoring* his business by coming in, and he felt his business and employees should *honor* their customers. "No problem" was not a statement that he felt reflected honor. The phrase "honor and serve" is now embedded in their values. They "honor and serve their customers, team members, and communities."

When reviewing your values, remember to reflect beyond what you want to see. Use this as an opportunity to clarify what you do NOT want to see. Often, we can uncover the real value and behavior in thinking about the stuff that's making us cringe today when we see it.

Are values and behaviors being demonstrated by your employees?

Do your employees *really* know the values of the business and what's expected of them? As business owners and leaders, sometimes we forget. We know what's important to us and the business, and we *assume* that since we know, everyone else does too.

We have worked with clients who felt strongly about their values. We had one client very adamantly tell us that their values were clear and that her team knew them. We heard, "Yes, we have values in place.

Yes, we talk about them consistently. Yes, employees know what they are. No, we do not want to have any additional conversations about values."

We encouraged the leader to ask the team of senior leaders about the business's values and the behaviors within those values. The leader cringed, and we assumed she wouldn't ask. In our next call, the topic was brought up again. The leader shared that in a meeting with direct reports, she asked the question about values. To her surprise, the leaders didn't know and couldn't list the values or how they were demonstrated in the workplace.

In other situations, clients say their values are defined and reviewed regularly. However, when the leader looks around, employees do not demonstrate behaviors that align with their values. Employees are behaving in ways that undermine or undercut the culture and values of the business. You may never make that connection without stopping to reflect on the behaviors of the values you WANT compared to the behaviors you see in the company. This happens more regularly than you might expect. When the values lack connection to behaviors and processes that don't reinforce the values in the business, they are easily forgotten and misunderstood.

STARTING PLACE #2:
YOU HAVE NOT IDENTIFIED YOUR VALUES YET.

Most of the clients we work with are at this starting place. It may be because, in some cases, they know in their minds what they value but have never defined it for others. In other cases, they may be a second or third-generation business owner and continue to do what's always been done, more accidental than intentional. Yet, in other instances, they may not see how identifying the business's values will impact the business results. In any of these instances, there are a few specific steps you can take to define your intentional culture and values.

- Think of your rock stars, your high performers. What are they doing? What behaviors are they demonstrating that you appreciate?

- Think of your lower performers. What are they NOT doing? Or what are they doing that drives you crazy?

Look for themes. Are themes emerging from these behaviors? You may notice your rock star employees consistently greeting customers by name, helping them find what they need, and carrying bags to the car. Maybe they also do this same behavior for their team members – asking them if they need help and offering to cover shifts if team members need time off. If those are the behaviors, what is the theme? Teamwork? Service?

This process helps you begin to narrow down the focus to the critical values of your business first. While this is a good start, it doesn't end here. Now it's time to get even more specific and think about how you and your team have demonstrated these values before. Think of this as story time. What are the examples of your team going above and beyond for a customer or team member? What happened in that situation? Why does it stand out? This is your brain dump time, so break out the flip charts or whiteboards.

For each of these values, think about examples where you or your team members haven't acted in alignment with these values. These, for us, are the "ugh!" moments - they aren't exactly the ones you're proud of, but they illustrate what you want a behavior to NOT be within your business.

The thing about culture, values, and behaviors is that specificity matters. It's important to define the behavior to the level that all employees (managers, supervisors, and entry-level employees) know precisely what behaviors align with the values and which do not. As we discuss the next steps you can take to define your culture, we will ask you to get specific.

12

What does this look like? Let's break down an example. Several of our clients have some element of retail or very customer-facing roles, so one of the most important values for their business is how they serve their customers. That said, customer service to you might look very different to someone else. As the business leader, it's up to you to define what successful customer service looks like for your business.

For many businesses, especially our clients in more rural areas, having a personal touch to their service is essential. This shows up as knowing the customer's name and goes even further to knowing a little more about them - about their farming operation, their pets' names, and the like. Why? This information is critically important for employees to be best equipped to make recommendations and determine what their customer needs and make recommendations, even if they don't know they need it or have it as an option.

For some, customer service means getting out from behind the counter. One particular business leader was frustrated that team members seemed to stay stationary behind the counter (demonstrated by more time spent on their cell phones, too much chit-chatting with co-workers, and not enough of that time spent with actual customers). He was considering removing the counter completely and equipping team members with mobile point-of-sale systems. Hence, there wasn't a counter at all, and team members would have to be out on the floor interacting with customers.

Another value that shows up frequently is integrity. Even integrity is a value whose definition looks different from business to business. To some, it's doing the right thing every time (even when no one is looking), and to others, it's about being ethical in all transactions. In this exercise of breaking the value down to specific stories and examples, we want you to start seeing the behaviors that come to life. These behaviors will serve as the north star for all of your other HR processes and practices within your business. These behaviors are the glue.

A word of caution.

Often, many business owners and leaders start to use common words for their values. Teamwork, integrity, innovation, or customer service are examples of commonly used values. Without clearer, more specific descriptions, they are too overused, too vanilla, too blah. They look like the values you see in every other business you walk into or visit. There are two critical problems with this.

Problem #1. If you use common words without specificity, people will apply their own meaning and their own behaviors to those values rather than the behaviors you identified. They assume they know what you mean because of their own interpretation and what they think it means or how the values show up. Something unique and specific makes it more memorable and encourages employees to understand what you mean by the value and the identified behaviors.

Problem #2. The values must sound like you. Use the words you normally use. Make them personal. Make them your own. Think of the business owner we mentioned earlier whose pet peeve was employees responding with 'no problem.' As he described it to us, he shared that he was honored customers chose the store. In addition, he wanted to make sure they were truly serving their customers, going above and beyond. At first listen, off the top of your head, it sounds like customer service. There's the value. Here's where you take it a step further. We used his words: "We honor and serve our customers, employees, and communities." Honor and serve were the behaviors to demonstrate his version of customer service. It has a more significant impact, doesn't it?

IT'S YOUR TURN

It's easy to keep reading, and think you'll work on your values and behaviors later. We'll guide you through this right now while it's still fresh and top-of-mind.

Step #1: Set a timer for 5 minutes. Think through the things you value in your own business, whether they are already defined or not. What are they? List them all out. There isn't a right or wrong, and there will be time to edit later. The goal here is to get them out of your head and onto paper.

Step #2: Here's the fun part. Now set your timer for 15 minutes. Review each of the values you wrote out, and jot down 3-4 stories or examples for each one. These might be stories or situations that have come up where these values have been tested (positively or negatively). Get as specific as possible because we'll use these examples to look for particular behaviors later.

Step #3: Timer's up! Put your pencil down! Read through your examples and review these questions:

- How did these examples support your values (or not)?
- How do your team members show these in their work?
- What do you WANT these to look like in your daily work life?
- What are the behaviors that really irk you or drive you crazy? Chances are if a behavior is driving you crazy, it is likely violating something important to you.

What do you notice emerging as you reflect on these values?

It may seem like a lot of high-altitude work right now and may even seem like it doesn't touch the day-to-day much. We will use the work you have started in this exercise as you build your HR and people practices. When you reinforce values and behaviors through your recruiting process, employee onboarding process, rewards, and feedback, your values and behaviors will begin to live in your organization. The consistency in reinforcing the values and behaviors you WANT is how you can guide your culture in the direction you want to see your business.

(Not only that, but the clearer we can be on values and behaviors now, the easier it will be for you to reinforce them in your other processes later. We'll show you.)

Let's dig into your values a bit more. What list of 5-7 values did you come up with from the earlier exercise? How would you describe this value in an action statement? For instance, "We have fun in our work every day" could be the description of your value for fun. Does it seem pretty straightforward so far? Good!

Next, start boiling this down into what this DOES and DOES NOT look like. Sometimes it's easier to start with what "does not" look like first, mainly because your annoyances and pet peeves in the business are likely violating one of your values.

Value	Description	DOES look like:	DOES NOT look like:
Integrity	Doing the right thing every time.	Correcting a mistake with a customer to preserve our relationship with them. Giving clear, honest feedback to team members rather than trying just to be "nice."	Giving critical feedback to one another without the intent to help them grow and develop. Taking shortcuts in our safety protocols just to meet customer or business needs.
Customer Service	We know our customers, and they trust us to help them.	Greeting customers by name, genuinely asking about them and caring to help them. Being honest with our recommendat-ions to them, helping customers understand why we may suggest something for them.	Making suggestions to customers for the sole benefit of our business if it doesn't truly help our customers. Not coming out from behind the counter to greet customers. Giving more of our attention to our phones and employee conversations than to our customers.

Like we've said, your pet peeves in the business most likely are symptoms of behavior violating one of your values. What are yours? What are the little things that frustrate you at the moment but don't necessarily seem big enough for a significant response? What are the patterns around them? Get as clear and specific as you can as you think through these - how is it an example of what you DON'T want to see?

After completing this exercise, you are 90% finished with identifying your intentional culture, values, and behaviors. This is a time to step back -- put them away for the day or a few days. Think about them as you go through the next few days. Are there behaviors you are seeing that aren't included that should be? Are there behaviors you know that you want to make sure are identified in the "what the value is NOT" column?

The most important step in completing this will be getting buy-in from your leaders, managers, supervisors, and employees. We will discuss this more in Section 2 when we discuss managing change.

CHAPTER 3:

WHO "OWNS" CULTURE?

I remember a location I worked in years ago and led an HR team. I formed an employee engagement committee to build up our culture and relationships between management and employees. Our committee intended to find ways to create better relationships between our production team members and everyone else typically referred to as "the salaried team." This particular location was unionized, and when I shared information about this committee with the union's business agent, his comment back was, "Oh, so you want to start a culture club?" (If you want bonus points, go ahead and get "Karma Chameleon" on your next playlist as an homage to Culture Club - I can assure you my business agent was not aware of his musical reference here).

But really? This was just one of the countless ways HR was perceived as the "owners" of an organization's culture. "HR" is often also perceived to be where employee survey data goes to have elegant action plans developed, so engagement improves. I'll admit, early on I fell into that trap, too. I thought the ownership of engagement rested on my shoulders, in HR, and that meant I had to swoop in and be the hero.

Yet something was missing between *my* plans and the *reality* of an employee's experience. I could see specific teams where there was almost no turnover and others where I couldn't hire people fast enough—in the same location. Why? Because of the leaders.

We work with many clients, small businesses, and family-owned businesses. In many cases, the business leaders and owners felt like I felt; that they were entirely responsible for the culture.

Many are surprised to hear that 70% of the variance between a strong and lousy culture is the employee's team leader's knowledge, skills, and talents, according to the State of the American Manager report published by Gallup. As the business leader, you can define the culture and be intentional about the culture you want to create within your business. You can do all of this, AND if there are leaders between you and your employees, you have less than 30% of the influence in whether or not your employees experience the culture you have defined.

It's also more than just the business owner or executive leader that needs to understand this statistic. It's critical for the team leaders and managers to understand this, too. In these same businesses, these same clients, the team leaders and managers think the same way - that the engagement and culture is "owned" by the executive leader. Often, the team leaders and supervisors' managers see the business leader or owner in the business every day and think, "I don't own the culture. That's what they do.

A lot of our coaching time is spent with managers, supervisors, and leaders discussing this 70% variance. We clarify that the role of the business leader or owner is to define the culture, identify the values and behaviors, and embed these values and behaviors in the business's practices. For the culture and values to come alive in the business, we need managers, supervisors, and team leaders to drive it, hire and recognize employees who demonstrate the values, and hold employees accountable when they don't.

With this in mind, the next step is key to culture. It involves identifying the expectations of your managers, supervisors, and team leaders to make the culture and values come alive.

CHAPTER 4:

DEFINE LEADERSHIP EXPECTATIONS

Leadership expectations are built on your values and behaviors and take them to the next level. Once you have defined your culture and identified the behaviors that support it, it's time to define what *your leaders* need to do to create and reinforce that culture.

We will talk more about job descriptions as we discuss specific HR processes and practices, but let's reflect on a typical job description for a manager or supervisor. Over the years, we have seen hundreds, if not thousands, of job descriptions. In most job descriptions for managers and supervisors, the list usually includes several bullets (often many, *many* bullets) on the operational responsibilities of the job, achieving the goals and results, and tasks one or two lonely bullets with something about "managing employees." More detailed job descriptions start to include a few more things like "to hire, manage, develop and retain employees." That's typically it.

We get it. We have small businesses, and there is no such thing as a role that solely leads people. All managers and supervisors are "working managers" and wear multiple hats. Most have responsibilities and tasks for which they are held accountable that are not related only to managing people.

Remember, the culture of your business *is at least as* important as your strategy and goals (as shared in the quote by Peter Drucker), and 70% of the variance between a strong culture and a lousy culture is the knowledge, skills, and talent of the team leaders. When it comes to job descriptions, the focus is often on the operational responsibilities, and the duties related to leading a team are almost a footnote at the end. As you define the leadership expectations, these will be included as responsibilities in the manager and supervisor job descriptions. There's more to these expectations than just a bullet point or a footnote.

We've seen patterns evolve through the years and our clients' work.

Here are a few common examples.

Values	Behaviors (How ALL team members are expected to behave)	Leadership Expectations (How leaders are expected to behave)
Integrity	Living the values of the business. Treating peers and customers equitably. Being honest and having the right intent. Doing what you say you are going to do.	Role modeling the values of the business. Giving honest feedback to employees. Taking ownership of the performance of your team Building trust with your team.

Teamwork	Making sure we have a safe working environment for ourselves and our team. Helping our team to achieve common goals. Sharing knowledge and information with the team.	Providing effective feedback. Recognizing employees for good work. Coaching employees who are not meeting performance expectations.
Growth	Looking for opportunities to serve our customers by being innovative. Being resourceful. Understanding the business, structure, goals, and strategies.	Encouraging your team to share ideas. Providing opportunities for your employees to grow and develop. Anticipating and identifying opportunities to change. Leading and facilitating change.
Service	Going above and beyond to serve customers. Anticipating customer needs. Listening to customer concerns. Providing solutions to customers.	Enabling employees to do their best by providing tools, advice, and resources. Listening to your employees.

Identifying and communicating leadership expectations to managers, supervisors, and team leaders is essential. Holding them accountable to meet those expectations is KEY. We can't stress the importance of this enough. Just as we embed the values and behaviors into crucial HR practices and processes for employees, we will do the same for managers, supervisors, and team leaders.

Here's the thing. It's hard. Yet if we don't embed it into our day-to-day practices, or into our leadership expectations, the culture we develop may not be the one we want.

LISTEN TO THE WINDS

You experience your managers and supervisors in a different way than employees experience them. The team, and the employees, have a different experience than you do. As the leader or business owner, you are one or two steps away from what is happening on a day-to-day basis. It's essential to stay in tune with what's really going on. Sometimes you'll hear rumblings and may want to pay attention to the silence.

Several years ago, in one of my first HR roles, I supported a crew of about one hundred employees on the 3rd shift. This crew had several supervisors, each there for many years and each leader had once worked the very roles that their direct reports were in.

As I spent more and more time with this team, getting to know the team members, their stories, and their experiences, I started to notice and hear the rumblings. They were subtle at first: team members hesitant to share anything negative, feeling they would be punished for doing so, looking at one another for approval before saying anything that might be potentially negative. Protective comments like "you didn't hear this from me" and "I don't want to get anyone in trouble" were commonplace. There was the shared mentality that they had their own culture (though I'll let you decide what kind of culture it was), trying to keep the day shift out of their business as much as possible.

The rumblings started with small, subtle comments about bringing ideas up in the past and team leaders ignoring them or not following up with them. They'd get louder every once in a while, and I'd hear more about how team leaders would treat employees and I would hear about how they were talked to individually (it wasn't respectful or professional). As I spent time with them, the rumblings turned into enough of a roar that I couldn't walk away without doing something. Even the director of this team knew something was going on but couldn't seem to get enough information to support it.

Eventually, we discovered enough reports of some team leaders mistreating employees that we could move forward and make changes.

I will never forget that night, pulling one of the crews of 25 employees together to tell them that we no longer employed their leader. I was expecting a pretty typical response, of very little response or reaction, where employees just went ahead with their night.

When we made the announcement, though, suddenly, the entire room broke into applause. I couldn't believe it and had to do double-takes a few times towards the director to ensure it wasn't just me being sleep-deprived on third shift. THEY WERE CLAPPING. As we dismissed the crew back to work, team members lined up and shook our hands on their way out of the room. To this day, it's one of the weirdest, strangest situations in my career (and I've seen some weird, strange things).

As I spent more time with the crew over the next few weeks, so much more came out of the woodwork. The stories, the experiences, the fear of bringing up issues to others who could do something because employees genuinely feared their leader. Those rumblings we heard? ...they turned out to be just the tip of the iceberg, the flag being tentatively raised to let us know something was going on without drawing too much attention.

Over the years, I've seen this play out time and time again. When leaders make the hard decisions to let team members (and especially supervisors) go - because they aren't creating or fostering the culture that the organization needs - **there is always more behind the woodwork**. What does this have to do with culture? If employees do not feel safe with their leaders, your best-planned strategies, plans and projects will be stymied from the start. Those leaders carry 70% of the influence on your culture, so make sure that 70% is pointed in the direction you actually want. Go further than knowing your values and take that time to break them down to the behaviors you want to see and DON'T want to see. As you make this part of your day-to-day discussion and conversation, the more you give all of your employees' permission to speak up about whether the values and behaviors are being demonstrated.

What do those rumblings sound like? How do you know if some of those rumblings are happening in your business? This list is only intended to help you be more aware of what's happening around you, and it isn't designed to make you feel paranoid about what is happening on your teams.

- Conversations between other employees get "shushed" or stopped when you're within earshot.
- You see more hesitancy in meetings when you bring up ideas for others' input.
- You hear more comments starting with "you didn't hear this from me, but..."
- Noticeable difference in others not sharing their thoughts or feedback (especially when they used to be more open with it).
- More sarcasm in responses.
- More turnover of high-performing staff.

Are any of these four-alarm fires? Not necessarily. I've found that simply paying more attention and being more aware of interactions can help me pick up when the winds seem to be changing. Does this mean that your culture is damaged beyond repair? Also no. Think of these as a blood pressure check; it doesn't tell you exactly what the problem might be (or where), but it gives you information and tells you that it's time to dig in further for more information.

With culture, especially in a young or small business, it's easier for leaders to stay close to each employee and reinforce their values and behaviors with your team - mainly because it's just you communicating the message. As your team grows, your managers or supervisors will carry more of this responsibility to their own team members. As a result, the risk increases as to whether your message, intention, and goals get diluted or misinterpreted by the leader. It's almost as if your message goes through the game of telephone, where you're whispering your message of "We do the right thing every day!" to your manager or team. By the time it gets to their employees, and further down the line, the message may sound more like "Win no matter what every day." It might not be far off from your original message but may reinforce behaviors different than what your values intend.

The clearer you get on defining the values of your organization and the expectations of your leaders, the less telephone you see in your teams.

CHAPTER 5:

BRING YOUR CULTURE TO LIFE

Why spend all this time thinking about values, behaviors, and culture? Frankly, we've seen too many instances where business owners and leaders spend time discussing their values and culture instead of living them. Defining culture and values creates energy and enthusiasm in teams. Soon after, the work gets shelved and forgotten. Later, we start to feel like something is "off" in our business - our turnover is increasing, our managers don't seem equipped to handle employee issues and concerns very well, and the business goals are not being met.

Our goal for you is to bring these values, behaviors, and culture to life, reinforced by your actions and practices. Our goal is also so that it isn't just a fun team-building activity we did "that one summer at an off-site event." This doesn't mean that you're constantly updating this information for your organization every month. **This means making it live through your processes and practices by connecting it to the goals, to how you hire employees, how you choose to reward and recognize good performance, and how you address poor performance**.

That's where we're going in this book. One of the best investments you can make is in taking the time to be *intentional* about what your culture looks like in your business. Not just how you want it today, but tomorrow, too. Investing the time, by yourself and with your leadership team, to get specific now will make the rest of the work easier. We'll demonstrate step-by-step how you can use this information to build more robust recruiting practices. We will show you how you can build on this to give your employees more actionable and improved feedback. We will show you how you can make this an everyday part of your business and communication. All this so that your employees are less interested in looking at other jobs - because your company has such a great culture.

This is the time to invest in your business culture. Remember, you already have a culture in your business today - but is it the culture you want to see tomorrow?

Let's start building the culture you want!

WHEN SHOULD I START WORKING ON CULTURE?

It may seem silly at first to start working on this. Maybe it's just you in the business, or you and one other person, talking about your culture and the behaviors you want to see may seem preliminary. This reminds us more of the response to business leaders asking when the right time is to make their first hire, where the answer quips, "before you think you're ready." Why? Investing today to outline what's in-bounds and out-of-bounds with behaviors, the easier it will be as your team grows. You'll never feel like you have enough time, and you have even less to put thought into it when your team is already taking your direction to make the business work.

I'll admit it, we were only daydreaming about building a team and a business when we first started talking about culture and values as People Spark® Consulting. Even before we left our corporate jobs, we outlined what values and behaviors would be most essential for us in our business: Staying curious, simplifying complex concepts and processes, having fun. What's been so interesting is how frequently we go back to evaluate whether we are staying aligned to these. It gives the bumpers in your bowling lane to keep you going in the right direction.

In the beginning, what you put down on paper does not mean it's the only time you'll work on this - you'll find that the behaviors to your values may get more specific and clearer with time. You may also find that there are a few values that you choose to edit or others you choose to add as your business grows and evolves.

It gets fun, though, when it's time to start building your team. This is when it's time to put these to work in how you talk about your company and the role you're creating and use these values and behaviors when assessing candidates. We'll take you into this further when we get into Recruiting and Interviewing, so give yourself the permission to take the time and start creating these values now.

The focus on an intentional culture, including values, behaviors, and leadership expectations, is the HOW; How we want to show up and how we want our employees to show up. The other side we need to cover is the WHAT—the WHAT is what we need to accomplish - our strategies, goals, and key performance indicators.

An interactive worksheet to assist in identifying your values, behaviors and leadership expectations is available at www.peoplesparkconsulting.com/bookresources. The worksheet also includes additional examples of values, behaviors, and leadership expectations.

CHAPTER 6

DEFINE YOUR DIRECTION

While our focus started on culture, it doesn't minimize the importance of having a good strategy and identified goals. We need to have both. Let's spend some time talking about goals.

In our work, we have found that many business owners and leaders have a general idea of the goals they want the business to accomplish. They have a sense of what needs to happen by the end of the year to consider it successful.

The thing is. . . a general idea is not enough. A general notion leads to wandering goals. Strategies, goals, and performance indicators should be clear, so the business owner or leader KNOWS when they have achieved it. These are the arrival signs to know you've made it.

If a business owner or leader is not crystal clear on the strategies, goals, and objectives, then managers and employees will not know them either. There's a compound impact here. If managers and employees don't know the strategy, goals, and objectives, they cannot work together because they don't know what success looks like.

Research shows that having clear and clearly articulated business goals boosts employee engagement at all levels. It keeps people focused and motivated. It provides a roadmap so people can track their progress—individually and collectively—and see how far they still need to go. Perhaps most important, it enables employees to make choices and take specific action to achieve meaningful, tangible outcomes.

Imagine running a marathon with no clear finish line. Slogging away, mile after mile, with no end in sight, is both tiring and tiresome. As someone who's completed one before, I can tell you I would have quit miles before the finish line had I not had a clear end goal. That last hill on the 25th mile...forget that!! But when I knew that the finish line was just around the corner, it helped me stay focused on the goal This is precisely how employees feel when business goals are general or vague. When you set and clearly explain your business goals, you may be surprised at just how quickly the finish line is in your sight.

In 2009, scientists in the Multisensory and Perception Group at the Max Planck Institute for Biological Cybernetics in Tübingen, Germany[1], presented the first empirical evidence to show that people walk in circles when there are no directions or landmarks to guide them. Think of people in a field, told to walk in a straight line with nothing to guide them in a straight line but their own intuition: no sun, no moon, no landmarks, no guides. The study found that people, thinking they were walking in a straight line, were actually walking in circles. Most interesting, walking in circles as tight as 66 feet. People need reliable cues to help them walk in a straight line: the goals *you* set and communicate!

Now think about this in terms of your employees. As a business owner or leader, you might say, "we need to head north" (if that's the general direction you want to go). Employees could agree and say, "yes, let's head north." Then, with all the best intentions and hard work, they head in the direction they think is north but end up walking in circles. You are frustrated because you can't understand why your employees aren't headed north. Employees are frustrated and tired because they

---

1   *https://www.mpg.de/596269/pressRelease200908171*

34

are working hard to head north, not realizing that they have been walking in circles for months.

What are the cues you've been sharing with them? How reliable and specific have they been?

Here's a question for you: Are YOU clear on your goals?

Business owners and leaders typically answer that question with a resounding "YES!". When we dig further, though, we frequently find that the goals are not as clear as they believe they are. Understandably, the team isn't clear on the goals either. If the goals are murky, how the business plans to achieve them will be even more so.

You may instinctively know your goals, but are they truly defined? To find out, try answering these questions.

- What are the business goals for the year? Get specific.
- What does success look like? How do you know when you've arrived?
- What metrics are you tracking to measure success?
- How often are the metrics reviewed and tracked?

Take a moment here to write down your answers, getting as specific as you can. Go further than stopping to pause and answering them in your head. Put it on paper.

Now reflect on what you wrote: Are you clear? Are the goals clear? Could someone (not you) read this and understand what the goal was?

Here's the next level: How clearly do your managers and employees understand your goals?

Many business owners or leaders assume that managers and employees are clear on the goals, and this assumption has too often been wrong.

To find out if your managers and employees really know the business goals, ask them. You may be surprised by the answers. In our experience, some managers say, "I think the goals are ...." That clearly indicates uncertainty. Others give answers like "grow the business," "make money," and "serve our customers" that are so generalized they could apply to any business. The intent here isn't to "catch" anyone doing something wrong; it's to check how deeply your goals are understood in the business.

We conduct HR assessments with our clients, and, as you can expect, we ask about goals specifically. The comments we included above are the most common answers we hear. We even hear these frequently from senior leaders, members of leadership teams, key managers, and long-term employees. In the rare event that a manager or employee knows the business's goals, it's stated word-for-word and memorized, not necessarily shared with any understanding of how their work helps achieve its goals.

What should you be listening for? If you aren't getting specific answers about company goals, you've got some more work to do. You are not alone. The good news? Clarifying your goals and connecting them to your team's work can start shifting things quickly.

One client worked hard to identify and clarify goals with his managers. He established goals at the beginning of the year, and he met with his leaders each quarter to discuss the goals and plans to meet them. He felt confident that each manager was clear on the goals based on the process they followed. When we asked the managers questions about the business goals, the responses we received were blank stares and silence. The business owner was horrified, embarrassed and understandably upset. All his energy and work were meant to establish and focus managers and employees on business goals. Yet the managers weren't able to state the goals. If managers can't talk about the goals, how can they provide that direction and focus to employees?

He's not the only one. In many cases, well-intentioned business owners and leaders want to provide this direction and focus to managers and employees but struggle with how to do so. Here are a few examples of the reasons leaders hesitate and struggle to be clear in their goals.

HESITATION #1
CLEAR GOALS WILL DRIVE THE WRONG BEHAVIOR

With one particular business, we could sense hesitancy in the conversation as we asked about goals. It started by asking about goals, not getting clear answers, and asking deeper questions. When we talked with individual leaders, they provided the answers, but each of their statements had qualifiers. They would start with, "well, this is the goal we have identified with the Board." Notice the qualifier? It was not a clear "our goal is...." That was the first indication the business goals were not clear enough to provide direction for employees. The goal identified with the Board was not consistently the goal communicated to the business as a whole.

As the conversations continued, we kept hearing more and more qualifiers. "Well, we have a goal to increase profitability, but as we increase profitability, we need to make sure we are acting in the best interest of our customers." Then, "we have a goal to increase efficiency at our locations, BUT we also need to develop our employees." These qualifiers created confusion and a lack of clarity. It caused managers and employees to think, "so, where are we going? What do I need to do??" They felt like there wasn't one set direction - they were heading in ALL directions.

Consider this for a moment: As individual managers struggle to share a clear sense of direction in their goals, it becomes a significant challenge for them to communicate clear goals and direction to their team members. Remember the 2009 study that showed people need reliable cues to walk in a straight line? That's exactly what was showing up here. Because there weren't reliable, consistent clues, people were walking in circles throughout the organization.

The Hesitation: Business leaders were concerned that if they focused too much on the specific goal, the WHAT, their managers and employees would focus only on this at the expense of the HOW.

The Reality: Establishing values and leadership expectations are establishing HOW you want your leaders to lead, and your employees to work. When the HOW is identified, goals can focus on the WHAT without hesitation. Employees will increase profitability (goal) and act in the best interest of the customers (value). Managers will increase efficiency at their location (goal) and develop employees.

HESITATION #2
CLEAR GOALS WILL DEMOTIVATE EMPLOYEES

Another business we worked with struggled to define its goals. The company was going through a process to standardize its operations with an external agency with identified goals AND had given specific goals to their investors. Knowing this background, we thought this would be an easy conversation since they had already established their productivity goals.

The leaders' hesitancy came through when it came to getting the goals on paper and communicating to employees. There was a real fear in committing to the plans on paper, with lots of "What ifs." What if we have these goals and employees can't hit them? What if the employees think that we are only concerned about numbers and productivity and not about them as people? What if external factors impact whether we can achieve the goals? How will the employees feel then?

The Hesitation: The business leaders felt that having specific goals would demotivate employees if a "what if" happened.

The Reality: The ability to see and progress to the finish line is more motivating and engaging than no goals. With no plans or unclear goals, employees will feel like they are treading water, running in place, walking in circles, and using energy but not sure to what end.

Now, let's talk about how to set clear goals.

CHAPTER 7

ESTABLISH YOUR GOALS

We are ready to set concrete goals for our team and provide reliable cues, so we don't keep walking in circles. Like us, you've probably seen all the tactics and methodologies about how to set goals as well. There are Rocks, the ONE thing, SMART goals, etc. There are so many tools and methods that you can cause writer's block by typing "set goals" into a Google search. Regardless of your process or procedure, we want you to start here with this question:

"What would need to be true or have happened by (the end of the year / the end of the quarter / this month / etc.) for you to say it's been successful?"

Sometimes we miss the obvious because we get distracted by details, data, and metrics. Yes, those are all essential tools, and we'll get further into the tools shortly. Be sure you don't see the forest for the trees.

What would need to be true for you to say you've had a successful year? Depending on where you are in your business cycle, it could be several things: staying profitable for the year, launching a new product/offering/service, hiring team members, and growing into new markets. That success is what matters to YOU.

Once you have this part defined, it's time to put it to work. How you break this goal down into specific objectives is how you will be able to set it into motion with your team. Let's take the profitability goal as an example.

What are some of the things that impact profitability for you? Get the laundry list out and start putting it down on paper. Several of our clients have a retail element to their agribusiness, so some of the things that impact profitability include:

- Customer counts (the more these go up, the better likelihood of increasing sales)
- Ticket value (the higher the amount sold on the ticket, the higher the top-line revenue)
- Margin (the higher margin will indicate higher profitability)
- Shrink/damage (torn or damaged product means having to write it off or fire sale it, impacting the bottom line and negatively impacting margins)
- Employee turnover (higher-than-normal employee turnover means that we're training and retraining employees throughout the year in excess of our budgeted turnover, not to mention the costs - both visible and invisible - to keep recruiting and bringing new employees in.
- Product turn (the faster we are cycling through inventory, the better)

With your definition of what success looks like, what are the things that impact it? How do they impact it? How do you know?

The list can (and does) go on! You'll see we didn't get into specific things that were more behavioral at this time (like customer service, etc.). That's the next step.

LET DATA BE YOUR FRIEND

It's easy to play the old tapes of what works and doesn't work in your business. "We tried that before, and our customers didn't like it," or "We know these products don't work in our market." If you've heard yourself start a sentence like that, we give you permission today to stop immediately and ask whether it's true.

Start with these questions:

- How do you know?
- When was the last time this was evaluated?
- What were the findings?

Here's the point: deciding to move on a goal or an initiative (or not) without knowing the data behind it (as much as you're able to get) is like putting together IKEA furniture without instructions. You may have all the pieces and even have a good idea of how it fits together, and the chances are that without those instructions, you'll need to take something apart and re-do it because you've put it together backward. Truth be told, even with the instructions, you can still make mistakes and have to rework something. I'd much rather be in a position only to edit a few pieces than have to take the entire set apart.

In our example, if increasing profitability is the measure of success, then let's dig into what the data says today.

- Customer counts - What are your average customer counts today? How do those shift throughout the year (knowing there's seasonality to many retail stores)?
- Ticket value - What are your current ticket values? Is this a pure number, or do other factors skew it? How do ticket values change throughout the year?
- Shrink/damage - What is your business's monthly or

annual figure for shrink/damage today? What products or departments have the highest shrink?

- Employee turnover - What is your turnover today? Just get the number, WITHOUT trying to explain any of it away (as in, "oh, he went back to school," and "she just found a better opportunity"). Turnover is turnover for the purpose of this exercise today.

If you're starting to feel overwhelmed, this is the time to take a deep breath. Our intent for this exercise is NOT to make you feel bad or like there's no hope. Our objective is to face our truth today and know where we're starting from. As a colleague of ours said years ago, "You can't fall off the floor." From here, there's only one way to go - UP!

A word of caution: business owners and leaders can really get on a roll with goals. Once the ideas come to mind, the floodgates open. Pretty soon, we don't have a list of 5-7 goals or metrics. We have a list of 10-12 goals and metrics. We worked with one client who loved metrics (I mean, who doesn't?!). In one of our first meetings, the client shared spreadsheet after spreadsheet, graph after graph. The information was fascinating and provided great insight. Yet, as we spoke to other leaders and managers in the business, they were overwhelmed with information and weren't clear on the goals. They gave general responses similar to what we shared earlier. When we shared the findings from our assessment, the leader was shocked. How could his managers NOT know the goals of the business? The problem was that there were <u>too many</u> goals and metrics. There was too much information for the goals to be clear to the team.   -

Remember, the purpose of the goals is to provide direction and focus, to guide employees to walk in a straight line. The more goals on the list, the less direction and focus. When identifying goals, think quality, not quantity. When we have a few high-quality goals, we provide reliable cues to our teams, keeping your team from walking in circles.

LEADING VERSUS LAGGING INDICATORS

One way to stay focused on the quality of the goal is to think about its impact. We work with business owners and leaders to focus on *leading* goals/metrics *rather* than on lagging goals/metrics.

A lagging goal or metric is a metric that happens as a *result* of actions.

For example, profitability may be your overall business goal - to increase profit by 5% over last year. Profit is a lagging goal, though, and it will happen as a result of other activities. A leading goal is tied to the actions or behaviors that will ultimately impact your lagging goal.

When it comes to leading indicators, think about the actions early in the process; if you do enough, it will lead to the outcome you're after. I think about this with sales calls. If I know that I need a certain number of new contracts/customers, then I need to have a certain number of appointments made, which means I must have a certain number of outreach/cold calls to set the meetings. For example, if your goal is to increase the number of new customers to 20 this month, you may need to have at least 40 appointments with prospective customers. To get those 40 appointments, you may need to make at least 200 cold calls/outreaches over the month across your team. Your leading indicator is that 200 cold call/outreach calls are happening every month.

Leading indicators can sometimes seem so basic and obvious that we blow past them, thinking it needs to be different. What are some of the goals you have in your organization? The table below is intended to help you break down the plans to find your leading indicators.

Goal	How It's Measured	What Behaviors Do We Need to See?
Increase new customers to 20 per month.	New customer accounts set up.	Appointments scheduled (at least 40 with prospective customers)
Increase sales in the store by 10% this year.	Sales per ticket amount. Number of tickets per day.	Team members are trained and comfortable making product suggestions to customers. Team members ask customers, "what else do you need today?"

These metrics are the goals you want to achieve, and they are lagging metrics. The third column details the activity needed to meet those goals.

You can also identify leading metrics for those activities. For example, the number of cold calls made is the leading indicator or metric for achieving the new customer goal. It must be tailored to your industry and the prospect-to-new customer conversion rate. If the conversion rate is 10%, you need to make 200 cold calls (outreaches) to achieve 20 new customers per month.

BRING YOUR TEAM ALONG

I realized recently I completely fell into the trap we warn our clients about. Why do I share this with you? To let you know this is normal and to share my observations with you to help you with yours.

In 2021, we added team members to our own team. We spent LOTS of time thinking through the specific work and tasks that our team would do, clarified what success would look like for them, and started to put together job descriptions. We knew what work we (eventually) wanted these team members to take off our plates as we adjusted our own responsibilities to further business development. We were hesitant at first and asked all the same questions many other leaders do: *Was the business stable enough to ensure we could consistently pay them? Was there really enough business and work to support it?* In addition to these, we felt like we were under the microscope a bit as HR professionals (we should know better, right?!) - so making the wrong hiring decision would be a really crappy situation for us and our reputation.

So, we tip-toed. We took our time through the process and didn't rush it.

By the time our team members joined, it felt like we had been talking about the work they would do for months (because, well, *we* had). The thing is, we had only been talking about the work our team members would do with one another. Sure, we shared the job descriptions and what success would look like for them, and then we kept moving right along with the business.

During a one-on-one conversation with a team member, I felt like what I was sharing with her was just a task list. It felt particularly "to-do"-like, and with a level of detail that I was just handing something over to her. It didn't sit right with me and felt too prescriptive for me. Yuck.

I realized in all the onboarding, conversations, and getting to know one another, I hadn't connected the dots for her. She didn't understand how the work she would be doing contributed to how our business performed and succeeded. I'm not alone, either. In a 2018-2019 study by Ceridian, 44% of employees said they DON'T know how the work they do every day impacts the business. Nearly half. And here I was, someone who knows this statistic, NOT sharing this information with my own team members. Ouch!

I stopped myself in the conversation and backed up. I started from the beginning: how will our business earn revenue and client projects work? Then I got into more detail with her - that THIS was how the seemingly benign task I had for her would impact that project, affecting our revenue.

That light bulb moment also highlighted the importance and necessity of having business updates with teams. Sure, it's up to you how transparent you want to be with your team. We may share more than you do about your business, or we may share less. It isn't about how much you're sharing. You're sharing information important to your team and will help them know where they are. Because of this, we started monthly (and now bi-weekly) business updates as a team. The intent of these wasn't about the status of projects or what was on everyone's to-do list. The purpose was to show how our marketing leads to calls and other business offerings, which leads to the project work each of us delivers. We started at the beginning. We clarified where we wanted our business to go, the revenue we wanted to generate, how we planned, and how we held ourselves accountable for getting there every day.

So, where are you in this process? Do your team members know how your business makes money? Do they know what your goals are in the business? Yes? Excellent! The next step is to ask them *how* their work impacts these goals. It's okay if they don't know. Part of your role is to explain this. As the leader, you already see these connections and understand this. That doesn't always mean that your team does, though.

Where do you start? We've begun a worksheet below to give you some prompts on how you can connect those business goals and key performance indicators (KPIs) directly to your team members' roles. Key performance indicators (KPI) are the leading indicators you are measuring and monitoring that most impact your business goal. Down the left-hand side, write down the specific goals of your business. What are you trying to accomplish? By how much? Get SPECIFIC here where you can.

Next, think through the ways you can measure progress towards that goal. What are the metrics? What are the key performance indicators (KPIs)?

Finally, break down some of your critical roles in the business. In this example, we've used a feed retailer with several cashiers and delivery drivers. Go further here, and answer the question, "How can this role impact the KPI?" Think about what is within the scope and control of this position. How can that impact (for better or worse) the KPI associated with your goal? Remember to be specific here. This exercise is intended to clearly connect the dots for your team members to show how what they do every day impacts the business.

As you think through your goals, KPIs, and roles, you'll be better equipped to make this connection for your team. Why does it matter? As we give recognition and constructive feedback, the clearer we are on how roles impact our goals and KPIs, the easier it will be to provide! Don't believe me? Just wait.

Business Goal	How is it measured? What are the KPI?	Role #1: Cashier How can this role impact the KPI?	Role #2: Delivery Driver How can this role impact the KPI?
Increase top-line revenue in stores by 10% year over year.	Customer counts/day Average customer ticket Number of up-sells/day	Ask every customer about our featured or highlighted products. Observe customer selections and make recommendations for add-on sales. Greet every customer in the store personally (using their names where possible), coming out from behind the counter to ask how we can help them today.	Before driving the route, double-check orders to ensure accuracy for each customer. During delivery, greet every customer personally. Observe customer selections, share information about highlighted or featured products, and ask if we can get them more information.

Here's the thing: as business leaders and business owners, we're moving quickly - making adjustments, thinking about the next quarter or the next year, and developing contingencies for crazy market fluctuations. I've found that this exercise can feel like it is forcing me to slow down and be intentional, really defining how each role connects to the things most important in the business. Taking this opportunity today helps move your team forward WITH you, without them feeling that tasks, initiatives, and projects are coming at them with no rhyme or reason. You're connecting each person to how meaningful their role is in the success of your organization.

So far we have covered culture and strategy, through goals and metrics. You've laid the foundation. Now we need to build on it, communicate it, get our teams aligned and behaving in ways that reinforce the culture and lead to business success. To accomplish these next steps, you need to build strong relationships with your team. You need to have effective conversations with your team. You need to give them feedback. The focus in Section 2 is how to do that.

SECTION

ALL SPARKS REQUIRE THIS

CHAPTER 8

TRUST

Everything becomes more effective when high trust exists in an organization. When thinking about trust, it feels too big or broad and difficult to wrap your arms around. It can sometimes feel like you have trust, while other times, it may feel as if you don't. Your employees trust you, or they don't. It's hard to think about what you can do to change it.

Ken Blanchard says, "trust is built through a consistent set of behaviors repeated over time." This quote gives an excellent description of trust because it makes building trust actionable. It's no longer up in the clouds; the behaviors you do daily impact trust. If those behaviors are repeated consistently over time, your employees know what to expect from you, and it will build trust.

A few key behaviors will increase trust when they become replicable behaviors. These were found in an article published by Geoffrey James in Inc. Magazine. As you read this list, you may feel a couple of things. You may think that these are obvious, common sense. But common sense is not always common practice. You may think, yes, that is my intent, of course.

As you read these behaviors, reflect on your behaviors, your actions. Do you demonstrate these behaviors? Do you demonstrate them consistently? Do your leaders?

Coach. Don't command. This sounds easy. Of course, we want to coach and not command. Take a moment to reflect on how often you may command (regardless of whether or not it's your intent). We all get busy. There are things to do, customers to serve, bills to pay, and problems to solve. When we are in the day-to-day working really hard, it's easy to yell out an order or very quickly tell someone to do something. Then we move on. Maybe it's appropriate now, but we never step back, reconnect and use the opportunity to coach our employees. Don't worry. We'll focus a lot on coaching throughout the book.

Tell the truth. Most of the businesses we work with identify integrity and honesty in their core values. The behaviors of integrity and honesty are essential to the company and the intentional culture. And yet, as business leaders, we know that there are things we can't share or can't share fully at times. Telling the truth is more than not lying (but that's important!). It's about how you act with integrity in moments that you know you can't share or can't share everything. How you respond can make or break trust. Being upfront about what you can and can't share is a way to act with integrity in these situations. Saying, "here is what I can share, and when I can share more, I will." This can be especially difficult when a team member asks you a question point-blank and can also be a point for building trust along the way.

Follow through. We all have good intentions. And, as we mentioned above, we all get busy and we forget things, like following up. In my years of working in manufacturing, there were a few habits I picked up that I tried to implement in every place I worked. One of those habits was carrying my little wire-bound notebook in my back pocket. When I was on the floor, and a team member needed something or had a question I couldn't answer at that moment, I made sure to write it down. More importantly, I worked on reaching out to those team members to follow up and let them know the outcome (whether it was what they wanted to hear or not). Was I perfect? Not in the least. Did I remember to follow up every time? No. There are still times when I think I could have been so much better in my follow-up with them.

What I heard, though, when I went back out to share an update, was consistent: "Wow! I didn't expect to get an update on that," or "I didn't think you'd remember that." It wasn't a personal dig on me. It was a reflection of their previous relationships with leaders. These leaders didn't intend to NOT follow up with them. Their work loads, demands, and daily fires piled up and distracted them from the follow-up. Not following up took away the relationship with their employees and damaged trust.

Take blame but give credit. Taking the blame is typically translated to "don't throw somebody under the bus." Yes, that. As a leader, this is also about taking responsibility. We are responsible for the work of our teams, what is and is not getting done, and for creating an environment that supports our team and customers. This is an aspect of one of the eight engagement factors: "my teammates have my back." This is also about ensuring that we recognize our team members for their contributions and work. When working with clients, I say, "we did this..." or "we did that..." if it's something I did. If it's something a team member did, I say their name. It is a way to recognize your team for their work (which, by the way, is another one of the eight factors of engagement -- more on that later).

Don't badmouth. This can be another easy trap to fall into. You are at work, it's busy, another employee doesn't show up for their shift, and you get frustrated. You turn to another team member and share your frustration. The intent is to vent a bit and then move on. The message you are actually sending to employees is, I will complain about people behind their backs. The employees you are sharing this information with (the ones you trust) are actually hearing that you will talk about them behind their backs as well.

For better or for worse, team members are always watching how you choose to react and respond. Those moments of frustration can reverberate far longer than your initial frustration. Additionally, those reactions and responses set the tone for what is acceptable to you in your organization.

Walk the talk. We all laugh at the quote "do as I say, not as a do" because it sounds so ridiculous. Why would I not do something I ask someone else to do? And yet, we do, without even realizing it. I am consistently (like daily) telling my daughters to pick up their stuff. They walk in from school, leaving a trail of stuff, jackets, backpacks and shoes. I get so frustrated (and at that moment, I don't coach, I command).

Yet I noticed something the other day. I walked in and looked around. My jacket was thrown on a chair. I had not one but TWO pairs of shoes in the middle of the rug, and my purse, books, keys, and water bottle were on the counter. Ouch. How often has it been like this? Probably more than I would like to admit.

I recently talked with a business owner who was frustrated that his team wasn't showing up for work on time. He decided to install time clocks to know when his team was showing up. As I listened to this business owner, I learned HE didn't come to work at the time he expected his employees to report to work. Hold on a second. The business owner expected the team to show up on time to work, but he didn't "walk the talk." Sure, the time clock worked. The bigger impact is that the leader started to show up on time and role modeled the behavior he needed to see from his team.

Listen more, talk less. Let's admit it: as business owners, and as business leaders, we are problem solvers by nature. In many cases, we got to where we are today because we move quickly, solve problems and move on to the next thing. We have been through a lot and have seen pretty much everything, so when an employee comes to us with a problem, challenge or question, our default is to solve it. We tell them what they need to do to get it done and move on. As a leader, we have been told that this is our job, right? Our job is to support our teams, solve problems, and remove barriers. However, all this problem solving (with the best intentions) impacts our employees differently. We end up doing a lot of telling and a lot of talking.

We devote time to listening and asking questions in our leadership development program. One recent participant (a senior leader with more than 30 years of leadership experience) shared his reflection after he started to truly listen to his team. He was surprised at how much more information he learned and how many better ideas he heard when he asked more questions of his team. He was appalled to think how much time he spent solving problems that he didn't need to, telling people what to do when that wasn't what they needed. He built stronger relationships and saved time and energy once he started to listen more and talk less.

Admit when you are wrong. This can be hard. As business leaders, we can feel like we need to know the answers. We feel we are not leading our teams effectively if we are wrong. Admitting you are wrong or admitting you don't know all the answers is a way to build trust, not erode it. If you acknowledge when you are wrong, you may find your employees trust you more. As leaders we must also encourage our team members to admit when they are wrong. So, while the first part of this may seem easier (if you can acknowledge that you were wrong), the second part can be more challenging. How are you responding when your team members admit when they are wrong? Does your team feel comfortable

Make employee success your #1 job. Sometimes we hear from business owners or business leaders that this is great in concept, but their #1 job is truly for business success. Yes, agreed. Here's the thing. Businesses are successful when employees are successful. So begin making employee success your #1 job, and your employees will, in turn, make your business success their #1 job. And you can't do it alone – you alone cannot make your business successful.

Now reflect on your actions and your behaviors. How well do you do on these behaviors? Think about it, honestly. And as you think about it, separate your intent and think about the impact of those actions, those behaviors. If we reflected on our behaviors based on our intent in those behaviors, we would probably all look pretty darn good. Considering the perspective our employees see and the impact on them may tell a very different story.

CHAPTER 9

INTENT

"People don't question your words. They question your intent."

- Joseph Grenny

This is such a great quote by Joseph Grenny, one of the authors of the book, *Crucial Conversations*. It all comes back to trust. We tend to think that people don't trust our words, when the truth is they may not trust WHY we are using these words or WHAT our genuine intentions are. Think about that.

Think of two people in your life, professional (preferred) or personal. First, think of one person who you trust, without a doubt. Now let's say this person came up to you and said, "I have some ideas for your business that I want to share with you." How would you feel? If it's someone you trust, you would probably think, "yes, I want to hear it. Tell me your ideas."

Now, think about someone you do not trust. If this person came up to you and said, "I have some ideas for your business I want to share with you," what would you think? Probably not anything good. You would question WHY they were sharing or WHAT they were going to get out of the conversation - the "what's in it for them?".

Both individuals are using the exact same words. It's not the words used that cause a different response or a different feeling. It's the intent. With the person you trust, you know their purpose. They aim to do the best for you and your success. Because you trust them, you trust that they have the best intentions. Whereas the person you don't trust, you are unsure of the intent, right? You might think, *Why is this person suggesting this? What are they hoping to gain? How is this going to hurt me later? What is their intent?*

Think about your employees and the importance of trust with your team. Throughout this book, we will share ideas, concepts, and language you can use to engage your employees and achieve business success. We will help you with the words to use. If your employees trust you, those words will positively impact them and not doubt you. They know your intent and know you have their best interest at heart. In turn, you'll help them stay engaged, which also helps you and your business.

If there is a lack of trust, your employees may question your intent as you start to use these words and tools. It may take longer to build trust, so that employees no longer question your intent or wonder what is around the corner. The good news is that all the tools and skills we discuss in this book are trust-building activities. As you continue to practice and implement these skills over time, that trust will increase.

Time invested in trust-building activities is one of the best investments you can make, and our goal is to demystify it as well. If trust is a consistent set of behaviors repeated over time, then using the concepts and tools in the book will help you build trust with your team members.

Now let's go back to that quote from Joseph Grenny, "People don't question your words. They question your intent." If you feel that your employees may question your intent, the best thing to do is make your intentions very clear. Share what your intent is and what it is

NOT.

In the book *Crucial Conversations*, the authors introduce a tool called "contrasting statements." This is one of our favorite tools, and we use it daily, both at work and at home. **Contrasting statements** are two simple sentences; one clarifies what your intent IS, and the other clarifies what your intent is NOT.

The first sentence, which clarifies your intent, is typically the easiest of the two to come up with. That's your purpose for having the conversation—the goal of talking to the individual or the employee. You want to ensure you are on the same page as your employee. And just as important, you want to ensure employees understand the process and expectations.

The second sentence, that clarifies what your intent is NOT, can be harder to verbalize. While it may be harder to verbalize, it's relatively easy to identify. It typically shows up as the pit in your stomach or that feeling that holds you back from having the conversation in the first place. Here are some of the common ones we hear from leaders:

- "I don't want them to think I don't trust them."
- "I don't want them to think that I don't appreciate them."
- "They do such good work, and I don't want to demotivate them."
- "I don't want them to think I am micromanaging them."

Say you have a strong employee, one of your rock stars, who made an error at work. They didn't finish a part of their required process, resulting in some downstream errors. You want to give them feedback, and you don't want the employee to think you don't appreciate all the work they do for you. The contrasting statements could be:

My intent is to make sure we have the same understanding of the process.

My intent is NOT to minimize the amazing work you do.

Or maybe you have an employee taking on a critical project for the business. You know they are capable, and it's the first time they have taken on this type of project.

My intent is to understand where we are in the project.

My intent is NOT to micromanage.

Think about situations you face. Where do you have feedback you need to share, but have been hesitant to do so? What is your intent? What is holding you back? What are you afraid the employee will think? Write out your contrasting statements.

As you practice this skill, use those very words.

My intent is…

My intent is NOT…

Repeat them, then practice again. Before long, they will start to flow in conversations without thinking much about the structure.

We have put this into practice for many years. We have a few tips on how to have the most impact with your contrasting statements.

- While we described them above as the first and second sentences, they can be used in any order. In typical conversations, we tend to start with the intent statement. "My intent is…"

  In situations where we are concerned that the person will be defensive or there is a lower level of trust, we tend to start with "my intent is NOT" and then end with "my intent IS."

- Whenever we share this tool, we find that people somehow want to connect the two statements. Unfortunately, they typically link two sentences with the word "but." What happens when you hear "but" in a sentence….an apology, for example? What do you think when someone says, "I am sorry, but. . ."? For me, the "but" negates the apology and tells me the person is not actually sorry. The same happens if you use a "but" to connect the contrasting statements. You contradict your first statement.

We have also found that people insert the word "however" instead of "but." "However," has the same impact. It's just a fancier "but." As a former colleague used to say, "However" is just a "but in a tux." Resist the urge to connect the two statements.

- Contrasting statements can be used at any time in a conversation. As a rule, use them whenever you feel your intent could be misinterpreted. For many discussions, this means right at the beginning. You may know that your intent will be misinterpreted based on the topic, individual, or past experience. The first two sentences of the conversation could be, "My intent is NOT…My intent is. . ."

In other instances, you may be mid-way through a conversation before realizing your intent is being misinterpreted. You think you are on the same page when the person you are talking to makes a statement, and you realize the conversation took a hard left somewhere. When you feel it's happening, use contrasting statements to clarify your intent mid-conversation. I was in the car with my husband a while ago, and we were discussing one of my upcoming business trips. I gave him ideas and suggestions that he could serve to our kids for dinner while I was gone. In the middle of the conversation, he said, "You know, I *am* capable." *Oofffff.* Did you feel it? The conversation took a sharp left. He was questioning my intent in sharing my suggestions. I used contrasting statements to clarify my intent by saying,

> "My intent is NOT to send the message that I don't think you are capable."

> "My intent is to give you dinner ideas with the food I don't like that you could serve when I was gone."

> (I am not so proud of the true intent either. It wasn't that I didn't think he was capable.)

Contrasting statements are also helpful because they can keep you from conversations that you don't need to have. There have been many cases where I have wanted to have a conversation with someone, and when I reflect on what my intent was for the discussion and what my intent is NOT, I have uncovered that I didn't have a good intention.

Contrasting statements might sound "too formal" or "too corporate" to you right now. If you resonate with either of these thoughts, I encourage you to hang with us. As you practice these, they'll become more normal and easier to say. You'll also find the ways you are most comfortable saying them. Sometimes my contrasting statements sound like "I'm not saying… I am saying this…," or a similar version. The words may shift, the intent stays clear.

Finally, if you still feel a little uncomfortable about contrasting statements, let me share this brief story with you. A couple of years back, we worked with an organization to deliver supervisor training to their team. A year later, I was having a conversation with their CEO as we talked about additional supervisor development. Out of nowhere, he said, "You know, I have a confession to make. When we learned those contrasting statements last year, I really had a hard time with it. When I first heard those, it just turned me off, and I tuned out. Recently, I was reflecting on this last year. Do you know what I've said more than anything else in the last year? 'My intent is…My intent is not…'" I had no idea as we went through the first training that he had experienced that, yet his response is one I know will resonate with others.

Try it on. Even if it isn't perfect, keep going. This tends to be one of the first tools our training participants begin using and one they begin to build momentum. We'll continue to build on this and add additional tools to help increase trust and your coaching relationships.

CHAPTER 10

LISTENING

"There is a difference between listening and waiting for your turn to speak."

Simon Sinek

I don't know about you, but that quote strikes a chord with me. I'll admit it. I have done it. I can feel it when I am preparing to respond to someone while they are talking, and I am not listening and don't fully understand their message.

We have spent lots of time with managers, leaders, and employees, talking about listening. Every single one of them have read about or learned the importance of listening, and can even retell specific actions they can take to listen more effectively. And yet, it's something most acknowledge they need to do even better. Us included.

Many people can perform a few common skills and actions well while listening—things like maintaining eye contact, using appropriate non-verbal communication, and asking questions, to name a few.

There are many more with which individuals struggle.

Avoiding Distractions. The most common we hear is

distractions. Think about how many distractions you have during the day, external or internal. Most managers and leaders struggle with external distractions: your phone, email, social media, and other interruptions (employees with a quick question or a problem they need you to solve). Additionally, you are dealing with internal distractions, the thoughts and ideas floating around in your head. *What time is my next meeting? What do I need to do next? Don't forget to respond to that email. Who's picking up the kids?* and so on. Each of those distractions pulls you away from actively listening to someone.

Not Interrupting. We interrupt for a variety of reasons: We are busy, we have heard it before, we have a great idea we want to share. We worked with a client on this topic, and he acknowledged how hard this is for him. It isn't that he thinks he's always right or that he thinks he's the smartest. In his case, he gets so excited about the topic and wants to share ideas. Regardless of the reason (whether well-intended or not), interrupting negatively impacts the conversation and the person we are talking with.

Having an Open Mind. We all like to say we have an open mind, but let's be honest, it's hard. There are many cases in which we don't keep an open mind. We feel like we have heard this story before (it's like a song on repeat), and we know how the story will end (we won't learn anything new). We feel we have tried a solution before or tried a new process. Sometimes, we think we have done this for so long that we just know.

Acknowledging Feelings. This is a challenging one for many managers and leaders. In some cases, it seems too touchy-feely, or you may get involved in conversations with which you may not be comfortable. We have had managers share that if they acknowledge an employee's feelings, it feels like they are agreeing with their perspective. (For example, if someone is struggling because they think a process is too complicated, acknowledging their struggles can make you feel like you agree that the process is too complicated). *Acknowledging feelings and agreeing are two very different perspectives.* You can honor and recognize feelings AND have difficult conversations in which you may not agree.

Being Patient. We are all busy. There is so much work, so many customers, employees, and tasks that need our attention. It can create an urgency that drives impatience. We can see the clock on the wall ticking away, and we quickly respond and move on to all those other things.

In many cases, we can be impatient for all the reasons we listed above - because we feel we have heard it before, know the ending, and are ready to move on. Tick, tick, tick. In my 20's, I participated in and led community service trips to Puerto Rico. We volunteered with a group of Dominican nuns in the mountainous regions. One rule for all participants was no clock and no watch (before we all had cell phones). At first, I couldn't understand this rule. What difference did it make? It turns out it was a HUGE one. I connected with and had such deep and powerful conversations while on those trips because I wasn't driven by time; I was driven by the relationships, and just being with people. I am not saying you can't wear a watch. I am saying to note how your watch (or clock) could be driving behavior that negatively impacts your interactions and your relationships. (Bonus points if you picked up on the use of contrasting statements here.)

In the moment, these actions, looking away, checking your texts, jumping in with a solution, or interrupting to share an idea, may seem small and inconsequential. But let's think back to the quote by Ken Blanchard: "Trust is built by a consistent set of behaviors demonstrated over time." These actions, however small or inconsequential they seem, are behaviors that are demonstrated and repeated over time. These seemingly small and inconsequential actions are the *exact* behaviors that can erode trust.

How about you? Reflect on your behavior while listening. When you think of how you listen to your team, how well do you do? What actions do you take to ensure you truly listen (and listen for understanding, not listen to respond)? What actions do you do well? What activities do you do that negatively impact the person you are listening to or the overall conversation? What impact do those behaviors have on the amount of trust in the relationship?

One of the ways I've found to improve my listening capability with employees and team members (while minimizing distractions, especially internal ones) is to give myself a "job" during the discussion. I will make it my "job" to summarize what I hear the other person saying in the discussion. It keeps my focus more squarely on the employee and not what's going through my mind so that when I do summarize, it's what they *actually* are saying.

To test it, when they've finished sharing what they want to share, I state, "What I hear you say is... (here's where I insert my summary of what they said). What am I missing?"

This does two things: 1) It keeps me focused on THEM during the discussion, not on me and my response, and 2) It allows my team members the opportunity to agree that I've captured their thoughts and have heard them, or to correct me if I've misunderstood something. While it may seem so minor, simply "feeling heard" is a primary reason employees choose to leave roles. When employees don't feel they've been heard or their experiences don't matter, they choose to look elsewhere. I'm guessing that isn't what you want in your culture, so I encourage you to try it out yourself.

Now that you have reflected on your listening behaviors, how do we know if we are doing it well? Here's our tendency. We focus on listening, truly listening to others. We walk away feeling like we did it. But did we? Who truly gets to decide if you listened? Do you get to make that determination? No. You don't. The person who gets to determine how well you listened is the person you were listening to. Because it's not how well you listened, it's whether or not the *individual felt heard*. That's an entirely different standard and can change how you think about listening.

A common quote we hear about listening and empathy is to truly understand someone's situation, "you need to walk a mile in their shoes." Yes. I agree. I'll add a perspective given to me: "to walk in someone else's shoes, you must first remove your own." And that is an excellent segue to our next topic, Empathy.

CHAPTER 11

EMPATHY

Years ago, fresh into a new role, I worked on building my budget for the upcoming fiscal year. It was my first time going through this process for this role, and there was plenty I didn't know. One of the reasons I accepted the move into this position was because of the leader, Scott. Funny enough, my last rotation had been at a location he led years before I was there. My team members, who had worked for him years before, always spoke so highly of him that I knew I couldn't say no if I had an opportunity to work on his team.

He was everything I had heard about—incredibly kind, thoughtful, and one of the most competitive people I had ever met. It was something that seemed like a juxtaposition for anyone else, but it worked for him.

Our budgets were due that day, and I had been sorting through spreadsheets from previous years' data, developing what I thought was a reasonable and appropriate recommendation for the year ahead. He needed my information to roll up his budget and so forth. I was nearing the finish line and couldn't wait to get this budget off to him, so I could be DONE with it.

Less than an hour before it was due, I reviewed it (for the 82nd time, at least it seemed) to make sure it aligned with my plans for the upcoming year and noticed that something was off. My budget wasn't just a little off, but about $150,000 off what we had submitted. I was instantly sick to my stomach. I felt like my entire career's reputation rested on this error and immediately started to tear up. I knew I had to bring it up to Scott, and I was terrified of how he would respond.

I dried my tears, went to his office, and took him through what I found as calmly as possible (I'm sure he could see the tear stains and bloodshot eyes quite easily by then). I didn't want to make him look bad or make our team look bad, and I felt I had let everyone down.

Scott didn't burst out with rage, he didn't chastise, and he didn't yell. He stayed calm, asked me questions, so he understood how we got to that point, and asked me what I had determined the next steps to be. He knew I already understood the impact - adding an extra $150,000 into his budget that needed to be justified at the last minute. He demonstrated empathy in the most textbook kind of way - by allowing me to get myself out of this situation, learn from it, and let me feel the disappointment I had with the error.

That's empathy - balancing your needs as a leader, the business, and your employees.-

The word empathy tends to be overused, and the true meaning is lost through that process. Empathy is a crucial aspect of trust, so let's discuss what empathy is and is not by contrasting empathy with sympathy and apathy.

There is a great visual of empathy, sympathy, and apathy. Think of a patch of quicksand (when thinking of quicksand, does anyone else's mind jump to the fire swamp with the Dread Pirate Roberts and the Rodents of Unusual Size? Or is it just me?).

If someone struggles in the quicksand, an apathetic response is not caring or not noticing and looking in a different direction. A sympathetic response is jumping into the quicksand to save them (without having a branch to bring you back up, causing you both to go down). An empathetic response is standing on solid ground beside the quicksand and throwing a rope to help the person out. We want to ensure we are doing as business leaders: standing on solid ground and throwing our employees a rope. How does this show up?

These responses, apathy, sympathy, and empathy, show up in our actions and words. Apathy tends to be heard in the harsher comments from managers, the horror stories you hear about managers. They say things like "do it because I said so" or "that's what I am paying you to do."

We saw this distinct difference in managers and leaders during the pandemic -- it was a learning experience for all of us. When the shelter-in-place orders ended, and businesses were beginning to open back up, many employees were hesitant to report to work. They had underlying conditions or lived with older relatives, and many were just nervous and scared about whether it was safe to return or not. We had some clients with managers that responded apathetically: "If you don't want to come to work, I'll find someone who does." Direct quote.

Other managers or leaders responded sympathetically. "Yes, I get it. Come back to work when you feel comfortable. It's okay." Notice how those managers were jumping right in -- they were not standing on solid ground because they needed employees to come to work to meet the business needs, to survive.

Empathy is standing on solid ground AND reaching out to help. An example of an empathetic response would sound more like, "I get it. It's uncomfortable right now, and there's a lot we don't know yet. Here is what we're doing to make it as safe as possible to keep the operation going. I want you to feel safe coming to work and know I'm doing what I can to make that as smooth as possible. Our customers need our business to be open, and I want you to know that we look forward to seeing you when you come in on Thursday."

In his book *The 7 Habits of Highly Effective People*, Stephen Covey focused heavily on empathy. He defined empathy as having high courage AND high consideration. High courage is standing up for what you want, need, or desire (or what your business needs). High consideration is having the same courage to stand up for what the other person wants, needs, and desires. Does this sound familiar? It's how Scott responded to me when I made my HUGE budget error. He held me accountable with respect and care.

Now, each of us responds differently in different situations. In some cases (like with my kids), I have high courage / low consideration. I tell them what they need to do and what needs to be done without really considering what that means for them. At work, I tend to have more high consideration / low courage. I ask questions and listen to understand and meet the needs of peers and team members, to the extent that I hold back on what I need or the business needs.

Whether you have high courage/low consideration or high consideration / low courage is not right, wrong, good, or bad. It's not a judgment call; it just means that you may not be getting the results you want or need to see. It also means that a high aspect (courage or consideration) is a strength. It's something you are good at, and it's essential. AND you need both.

Responding with empathy does not mean changing who you are. It means increasing the one that's low (courage or consideration). If you have high courage / low consideration, use tools and develop skills to increase your consideration. If you have high consideration / low courage, it's using tools and developing skills to increase your courage.

The good news is that the tools and skills we will discuss throughout the book can help you add this balance -- incorporating courage AND consideration into your interactions with your teams.

All of the steps you take to increase courage or consideration are part of continuing to build trust. Building trust with your team is a key aspect of business success, which is not surprising. Without trust, none of the other work we will do matters.

Remember, trust is built through a consistent set of behaviors repeated over time. The behaviors to focus on to build trust are the behaviors associated with being clear about your intent, listening, and responding with empathy.

The other work we will explore involves changes within the business to strategies, processes, and expectations. While implementing new things can be hard, getting teams to change their behaviors and attitudes to the new ways of working is even more challenging. We need to lead our teams through these changes for business success. That's exactly why we're heading into change management next. A downloadable resource with specific phrases you can use to increase trust, be clear on your intent, and listen to understand is available at www.peoplesparkconsulting.com/bookresources.

CHAPTER 12

MAKING CHANGES

I always dreaded projects when change management leaders were brought in during my corporate days. I never understood what they did. I'm sure I had some internal eye-rolling, too, when asked to join in some of the change management meetings. Along the way, though, what I learned made me much more of a believer in change management practices and the impact they can have on whether or not a change is successful.

Am I saying you need a dedicated change manager for initiatives or projects in your business? Nope. Not necessarily. I am saying that understanding how people react and respond to change, and knowing some practical skills to lead through it, can be the difference between having something that's regarded as "flavor of the month" by your team or something that sticks.

"THERE'S NO SUCH THING AS A SMALL CHANGE" (POSTER IN ERIN'S OFFICES SINCE 2008)

Here's the thing about change-regardless of whether it's perceived as positive or negative, as humans, we will all go through a fairly predictable cycle as we adapt to it. I've seen this for massive changes, like mergers or acquisitions, and seemingly benign changes, like installing handwashing stations for a food manufacturing facility.

There truly is no such thing as a small change. What looks or feels small to you will be a big, giant deal to someone else.

THE ELEPHANT AND THE RIDER

There is an excellent analogy to how people (ourselves, and our employees) respond to change—the analogy is the Elephant and the Rider. Jonathon Haidt created the concept in his book, *The Happiness Hypothesis,* which was further developed in the book *Switch* by Dan Heath and Chip Heath.

Here's the premise: Our brains have two independent systems working at all times. We have a rational system (the Rider), who is logical, deliberate, and planful. We also have an emotional system (the Elephant), which feels joy, pain, and pleasure. The Rider is looking at the long-term impact, the destination in the future, and the Elephant focuses on the short-term and instant gratification.

"The Rider provides the planning and direction, and the Elephant provides the energy." At first glance, it looks like the Rider is in control. The Rider holds the reins, telling the Elephant which direction to go. Even with this, the Rider is small in comparison to the size of the Elephant. The Rider can direct and pull the reins and give direction to the Elephant, but if the Elephant doesn't want to go, it's not going to go. Period. Have you seen or felt the Elephant and Rider conflict like this during a change?

We have too.

When implementing change, we must appeal to both the Rider and the Elephant. We need to address the logical Rider and the emotional Elephant. Therefore, we will address change management from both perspectives.

Let's address the Elephant first, the emotional side of change.

CHAPTER 13:

THE EMOTIONAL SIDE OF CHANGE

The Kübler-Ross Change Curve is a helpful model in managing change. It is based on the stages of grief, developed by Elisabeth Kübler-Ross in 1969 in her book *On Death and Dying*. I know it sounds rather morbid to talk about simple changes through the lens of death and grief, but there are more parallels here than you may think.

Every change we go through creates a sense of loss. It does not matter if the change is perceived as positive or negative, chosen by us or imposed on us, there is still a loss. It could be the loss of confidence (having to learn something new or different). It could be the loss of the known. It could be the loss of working closely with a friend.

As business leaders, this may be even harder to recognize in ourselves. We are the ones making the decisions. We are the ones implementing this change. And yes, we will also feel the feelings associated with a loss. Reflect on a change you recently made in your business. Maybe you changed your business strategy, maybe you had to let an employee go, maybe you had to adjust responsibilities. What was the loss associated with this change?

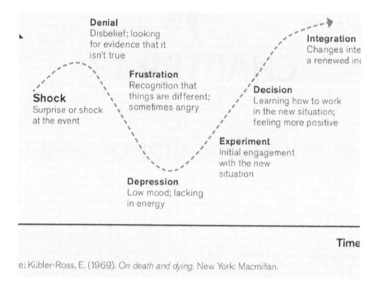

Denial
Disbelief; looking
for evidence that it
isn't true

Integration
Changes inte
a renewed in

Frustration
Recognition that
things are different;
sometimes angry

Shock
Surprise or shock
at the event

Decision
Learning how to work
in the new situation;
feeling more positive

Experiment
Initial engagement
with the new
situation

Depression
Low mood; lacking
in energy

Time

e; Kübler-Ross, E. (1969). *On death and dying.* New York: Macmillan.

These five stages of grief include Denial - Anger - Bargaining - Depression - Acceptance. In change, people experience these similarly, moving through Shock - Denial - Frustration - Depression - Experimenting - Decision - Integration.[2]

Here's the thing about these emotions and this change curve: while we would like people to move through this neatly, from left to right, quickly and predictably, humans do not operate in that clinical, sterile way. Remember, this is the elephant in all of us, the emotional side.

We use the stages as guideposts because the stages are fluid. We may find a team member is taking on a new change well and starting to experiment with the new expectations of their role really smoothly. When they make a mistake or run into a roadblock, they may move back to frustration or depression, with statements like "I'll never get this figured out!"

---

2   https://www.ekrfoundation.org/5-stages-of-grief/change-curve/

If you reflect on your own experiences of change, or the responses from employees going through change, you can start hearing what each stage sounds like. It's a helpful exercise to think about what your own team has said as they move through change. Not only is it beneficial to try and determine where they are on their transformation, but as you'll see a bit later, it gives you a data point to know what communication and information they may need from you.

Here is a snapshot of some of the phrases you may hear in each of the stages.

- Shock
    - No! I can't believe this is happening!
    - Have you heard?!
    - You'll never believe what I just found out.
    - Why would they think this was a good idea?!

- Denial
    - We've been through this before - surely they'll get this figured out before we have to move forward with this.
    - They'll never do that here.
    - There's no way I'm doing this.

- Frustration
    - I can't believe they're going to take 20+ years of work and just disregard it.
    - This is just ridiculous!
    - No one knows what they're doing.
    - This will never work out. I'll never figure this out.
    - This is just going to be another flavor of the month.

- Depression
    - When is this going to end?
    - I'm so tired of showing up every day, not knowing how to do my job.
    - It doesn't mean anything to anyone if I'm there or not.
    - Why should I even bother learning this?!

- (Silence)
- Experiment
  - Fine, if this isn't going to change, I may as well try to figure out how to survive it.
  - I'll try it to see how bad it really is.
  - I heard from the other team that it wasn't so bad after all, and some things were decent.
  - I'll give it a shot.
- Decision
  - This may actually work.
  - I found a way to do this better.
  - Do you know what I learned today?!
- Integration
  - Wow, I can't believe we survived as long as we did with the lack of systems/resources/people we had in those roles.
  - How was I even getting work done before?

The best way to determine where you or your team is on the change curve is to listen to the words you hear. Reflect on changes that you have made in the business. Maybe you implemented a new system, going from a paper process to a computerized process. Perhaps you merged with another business. Think of the statements and questions from your team. Did you hear similar words or phrases like those mentioned above? What were you hearing?

We had a client ready to announce that they were merging with another organization. There were NO jobs impacted by this - no cuts, no layoffs, nothing. Even though this change was expected to be positive all the way around, it was still a change. What was the first reaction from employees? "Do I still have a job?" SHOCK. This announcement still caused a response sounding like shock because they previously had no understanding that this was happening.

Over the next few weeks, the questions shifted from shock and denial into frustration and depression. This was more pronounced once the deal closed, and the team experienced even more change. Their point-of-sale systems had to be combined, their logos were updated, and many team members had new managers. Employees had to say the new organization's name out loud when talking with customers; not the name they'd been saying for the last 25 years. Responses from team members during this time reflected this, too.

"I'll never figure this out. I hate having to do it this way. I knew my way so much better. Why do we have to do it like this? Can't we just keep on doing what we were doing before?"

These stages - frustration and depression - are the riskiest points in change for your team members. They are at their most vulnerable in this space and are more at risk of saying "forget this!" and leaving. Your role as a leader is most critical to supporting your team as they work through the frustration and depression stages.

We worked side-by-side with these leaders through the transition, continuously listening to the words and actions of the employees. The leaders continued to guide and coach employees through frustration and depression, and after a few weeks, the language started to change. The team members were beginning to ask, "Do you know what I learned today?" and say, "I didn't know how to do this, so I dug into it further." Yes! They were moving to experimentation. We did a celebratory dance the day we started to hear things like, "I know others were struggling with this, so I shared a few of the tips I learned." Team members were not only beginning to embrace the new systems and processes; they were helping each other.

The leaders guided the elephant side of their team members. It took time, consistency, patience, and coaching. Today, they accomplish excellent results because the employees embrace the change and drive the business forward. Are all the employees? No. Some are still lagging behind the curve but continuing to move forward. Some have decided not to be involved and chose to leave, and that's okay. These changes aren't for everyone.

Now, we can't forget about the riders—the more logical and planful side in all of us.

CHAPTER 14

THE LOGICAL SIDE OF CHANGE

The commitment curve is similar to the change curve in that the goal is to support people through the process of accepting and implementing changes. We're guiding the emotional elephant along the path, coaching employees individually as they go through the change cycle.

The commitment curve helps you be more planful and proactive, logical and thoughtful in gaining buy-in to the change. It appeals to the riders. There are different versions and illustrations of the commitment curve, and here is a standard, short version of it:

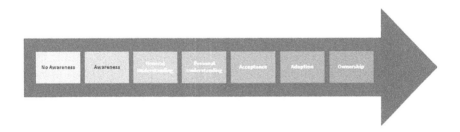

On the left, we have the stages of complete oblivion, where others have no awareness of the change. In the move from No Awareness to Awareness, communication with employees may trigger the Kübler-Ross emotional response to change to begin (remember, Shock is the first part?).

As we move the commitment curve to the right, employees gain a general understanding of the change. This often involves understanding the basics of what is happening, when, and why it is happening. At this point, your employees learn that there is a change happening, and even some of the basics of it, though they won't yet know how it impacts them personally.

The next step on the commitment curve is moving to personal understanding. This takes the starting change and breaks it down to the individual level to how the change will impact employees personally. Here is where employees learn more about what is expected of them in this new change, who is on their team, and what success looks like.

Further to the right are Acceptance, Adoption, and Ownership. This is where you start to see the magic happen. Team members are beginning to buy into the change in these stages and can wrap their minds around it. They are beginning to learn and practice the skills and behaviors needed. Team members see the light and support and encourage others to join them.

Think about it this way. To *really* impact change, you need to speak to someone's heart, head, and hands. In the early stages of communicating, in the shift from awareness to a general understanding, effective messages involve appealing to the heart, sharing messages about why this change is important, and what the benefits will be. You change minds (heads) as you move further through personal understanding and acceptance. By the time we get to adoption and ownership, team members are now adapting and are doing the different behaviors (their hands) and actions you need to see for the change to be successful.

In true rider (planful and thoughtful) fashion, there are questions employees will ask or information you will want to provide to best support them. These questions help you in several ways. First, if you are processing the change yourself, you can ask these questions to your leaders to help you move through understanding, acceptance, and adoption. Second, if you lead a team going through change, these questions will help you provide the information the team needs to support the change. You can anticipate the questions and build them into your communication.

When your team has no awareness or is just becoming aware, it's important to share information about the why and the big picture. Answer questions like "What is the change?", "Why are we doing it?", "Why now?" "What are the benefits?" and "What is the risk of not changing?" That last one is one of my favorites that many leaders fail to answer.

As employees move through awareness and need more specifics about what, share information that answers questions like "What is changing and what isn't?" "What is the timeline?" "How are decisions being made?" "What does this change mean for my team and me?" "What is expected of me?" and "What do I need to do differently?". Supporting team members by sharing what is NOT changing can put more perspective around the change and provide more stability.

We mentioned above that the most critical time for employees in change is the valley of frustration and depression.

> *"The more we can do to support people through general*
> *and personal understanding, the better we can help them*
> *minimize their time in the frustration and depression stages*
> *of the change curve."*

There's an important point to realize here. As leaders, we know that people will feel differently about any change. It won't be linear, and it won't always seem rational, either. People are people, after all. As leaders, by meeting our team members where they are, knowing what these changes mean overall and what they mean for them individually can minimize their time in the frustration and depression part of their change journey.

If you're trying to move employees...	Your communication should address these questions.
to Awareness	What is the change? Why are we doing it? Why is this change happening now? Who was involved in the decision? What is the risk of not changing? What are the expected benefits?
to General Understanding	What is changing? What isn't? What is the timeline? Who will be impacted? How are decisions being made?
to Personal Understanding	Where do I go if I have questions? What does this change mean to me? How will this change impact me? How will this change impact my team?
to Acceptance	What is expected of me? What do I need to do differently? What new skills do I need to learn?

This part (frustration and depression) of the change curve is the most dangerous for leaders. When team members are in this part of the curve too long, we see employees choose to leave. They feel so overwhelmed and frustrated that they can't see the way forward and may decide to go elsewhere entirely. At this point in frustration and depression, starting over from the beginning somewhere else seems easier than adjusting and adapting to the new changes coming at an employee.

Remember the story of the merger we shared earlier? The leaders needed to support their team members through the valley of frustration and depression. Our advice was to keep adding to the "General Understanding" message of the change. We stress the importance of explaining the WHY, the benefits to the organization, and the risks of NOT going through the change. You may feel like you're constantly repeating yourself with the why messages. Be okay with being the broken record.

This is bigger than making sure we are providing this information to our team members; it's realizing where we, as leaders, are in our own change process.

As a leader, we're privy to information in the business and can often see a few feet ahead of where our team members can. Picture this: Imagine you're driving through dense fog on a two-lane road at night. Your team members may only be able to see a foot or two ahead of their headlights. They are going slow because they can't see further ahead than this. On the other hand, you may have headlights or fog lights that help you see about five or ten feet ahead of them. You can go a little faster because you can see the road a little further out. Here's how this translates into change communication: As leaders, we can see a little further ahead and can see the path forward. We communicate from this place, too. We see that the road is safe. We know what to do, so we're ready to move forward at full steam.

Since our employees don't have the same information you do, they can only see a few feet ahead. They don't know that it's safe yet, and the path forward isn't as clear for them. They slow down, strain their eyes, and grip the steering wheel a little tighter to move forward.

Any kind of change works this same way. We're ahead of our team, waving them on to join us, yet they don't know it's safe yet. Then we get frustrated because they aren't moving faster and don't trust us and our plans. We tell them what they need to do to join us, yet they don't. As our frustration grows, we get more impatient with our team and start getting more direct in our statements - this is where the "because I said so" and "if you don't do this, I'm going to write you up" responses start happening.

Are you cringing yet? Think about times when this may have happened in your own career, either as an employee or a leader. Reflect on those situations. What was happening? What was being communicated? How were team members responding? What actions were they taking?

One of the most indispensable lessons I learned about change management is that we, as leaders, tend to communicate to our teams from the place we are on our change journey. We've had more time to absorb and move through the change ourselves (even if it's just a day!) than our employees, and by communicating with our teams from this place, we don't allow our team members to process through the change themselves. We force it onto them and expect it to work successfully and without resistance.

We worked with one client on initiatives to increase productivity. During an enthusiastic brainstorming session, one leader identified a fundamental change he needed his team members to make to help them hit their goals more easily. This leader was so excited about the change he started physically sitting on the edge of his seat, ready to take action. Where was this particular leader on the commitment curve? He was moving quickly and already in Acceptance, ready to move to Adoption. He was READY!! He was prepared to tell the team members what they needed to do differently and by when. He was communicating based on where *he* was, NOT where his team members were. Whoa! Stop the train.

We asked him to stop and think about where his team members were in the change. They had no idea that this discussion or brainstorming session was taking place. So where were they? No Awareness. None. What would have happened if he had communicated to his team then? All the feelings. The shock, denial, frustration, and potentially depression with all the other changes taking place. We paused, returned to the questions on the commitment curve, and started at the beginning. He formulated a message to his team based on where the team was on the commitment curve: talking about the change, why we were making the change, how it would benefit the team and the business, and how it was tied to the business's goals. Whew. Crisis averted.

In Section 2 we focused on building strong relationships with your team. We discussed the importance of trust and clarifying your intent, how to truly listen and respond with empathy. And of course, as we build relationships and refocus our team to our intentional culture and strategy, there is going to be change. The good news is that all of the skills and tools we discussed in Section 2 are also actions and behaviors that will engage your team (because we all want engaged and high performing employees). There are more ways that you can engage your team, specifically the eight factors of engagement we introduced at the beginning of the book.

A video with additional concepts associated with leading teams through change is available at www.peoplesparkconsulting.com/bookresources.

ENGAGING YOUR TEAM

Most books or models follow the employee life cycle. Starting at the beginning with finding new employees, bringing them on board, then rewarding and retaining them until they exit, whether voluntarily or involuntarily. Just like a scientific life cycle from the moment you arrive on earth until the moment you leave it. From the moment you join an organization to the moment you leave it.

We are not following that same model here. Business leaders typically don't start with looking at all of the HR strategies and

processes when they are considering hiring their first employee—
they tend to think about it after they have employees in place. They
start to believe it's time to have more structure or that it's time to
do something different to achieve their goals. At that point, you
have employees in front of you already. They are here. The best thing
you can do is focus on them first.

We will cover a lot of ground as we discuss engaging your team.
There is a lot to cover—all kinds of good stuff. As we get started, we
want you to think back to the introduction, where we talked about
the eight engagement factors.

If we were to boil it down to the most important thing you can do
to engage your team -- it would be to coach your employees. Yes,
coaching. It isn't that pizza parties and rewards aren't fun, or that
potlucks can't bring people together. It's that the biggest driver of
engagement centers around the trusting relationship that exists
between an employee and their leader. The intent here is NOT to
minimize all the other good information we will cover. The intent
is to share how much this one skill can have an amazing impact
on you, your business, and your employees. Seriously. A video with
additional concepts associated with leading teams through change
is available at www.peoplesparkconsulting.com/bookresources.

SECTION

3

SPARK ENGAGEMENT THROUGH COACHING

CHAPTER 15

COACHING IS KEY

*A*re you coaching golf or basketball?

A When I was in high school and college, I played competitive golf. In my state at the time (Ohio), coaches were only permitted to talk with their players at the turn; parents and spectators weren't allowed to speak with them at all. If I were in a 9-hole match, my coach could only talk to me as I walked from the 5th green to the 6th tee. For an 18-hole tournament, my coach could talk to me between the 9th green and the 10th tee. It might be a couple hundred yards on some courses and only a few steps on others. That was it. A tournament round could last between four and five hours, sometimes longer, and I could only spend a few minutes with my coach.

I was not the #1 golfer on my team; I had some great rounds, and I had some awful rounds. More often than not, I was constantly teetering between solid and going-to-lose-it-all on any given day. I remember many rounds where I frequently searched for my lost ball in the woods or prayed that I didn't lose another ball in the water. There were rounds I wish my coach had been there to see a shot, too.

On those rounds where I was teetering, it was up to me to stay focused, determine what was working and not working, and survive the round as best I could - all on my own. My coach had maybe three minutes to try and get my head back into the game if I hit the turn in a bad spot, and he couldn't sit down to process or evaluate what was working.

I also played basketball throughout high school and coached a local freshmen girls' basketball team in graduate school. Unlike golf, in basketball, coaches pace the sidelines as their players are on the court. They are encouraging and praising their players, making real-time adjustments to their plays, and helping their team anticipate what's coming that the players may not see. The coach is right in the game with them.

Coaching basketball was much more in line with my personality and background, though it isn't to say it was easy. Sometimes the coaching was pretty easy, like explaining the connection of pre-game meals involving Cheese Balls and Mountain Dew as a suspected reason my players had no energy for the game by the second quarter. Coaching was often a puzzle, not knowing which piece to try next. My team went on a losing streak for about six weeks; we would be so close and lose at the last minute. My team of seven 14- and 15-year-olds struggled through our 6AM practices as we survived the losses.

In one of our last games, I knew our team could win. We had played the other team before and knew we had worked on many things that had kept us from winning the first time. When we got to the gym and the game started, an alter-ego of each one of my players showed up. They couldn't dribble, wouldn't pass to one another, continued to turn the ball over, and stopped hustling down the floor for defense. By halftime, we were down about 15 points.

In the locker room at halftime, I told the girls that I was at a loss. Speechless. I'd seen them practice, knew what they were capable of, and didn't know who the team was at the gym right then. It wasn't the group I knew. As I got ready to leave the locker room, I told them, "You've elected captains to your team for a reason. I'm asking your captains to talk with you after I leave. You know what we need to do on the floor. You've practiced. You've worked hard. If you choose to join me for the second half, I want to see you out there bringing your absolute best." And I left.

The girls came out a little hesitant but ready to play a few minutes later. During that half, I still paced the floor, but I stopped shouting - encouragement <u>or</u> corrections. About halfway through the third quarter, one of my players (Meghan) came up to me and said, "Coach Erin, we don't like it when you're quiet on the sidelines. We like to hear you yelling; it tells us what we're doing right and what we aren't. Can you start yelling again?"

Her question and candor stopped me in my tracks, and I still am grateful for her courage to come forward. We didn't win that game, but we did win that half.

Ask yourself, "Am I coaching golf or basketball?" and, "What are the 'Meghan's' on my team asking me to do to support them?"

I recognize that sports stories and analogies can be overused when discussing coaching, and I agree that they don't fit in every situation or business. At the heart of these examples, though, team members are counting on you to let them know what is working and what isn't. They are also looking for your encouragement to help them grow. They might have the courage that Meghan did to ask for it or wander through the woods trying to find yet another lost ball through their tears and frustration.

Too often, I hear from employees that they aren't hearing *anything* from their leaders. Sure, they hear the "how are you?" and day-to-day information, but they aren't getting any information on what they should continue doing or what they need to correct. **Too many leaders coach golf when their team members want a basketball coach.**

THE TRAP FOR YOUR ATTENTION - WHERE ARE YOU GETTING PULLED?

One of the biggest traps out there is the trap for our attention. Often when we talk about coaching, people immediately begin to think about corrective action and giving constructive feedback, typically to our lower-performing team members. Letting our attention move there means we lose sight of our solid players and the attention and coaching they need.

Some Interesting studies show a high return on investment (ROI) for coaching. One study from CoachHub showed an ROI of 570%[3]. The results revealed that for every minute or ten minutes we spend coaching a team member, we would see a 570% ROI on that time invested. While this is phenomenal, other studies show that leaders typically spend *less than 10% of their time coaching* their employees. Why? Because they're bogged down in the other stuff, like juggling multiple tasks and dealing with underperforming employees. By spending more and more of their time on that "stuff," they spend less of their time where the ROI is highest.

In one of my last organizations, I got pretty excited about working with a sales team and accessing data to better understand and experiment with the typically anecdotal HR stuff that HR people would sometimes say. I wanted to experiment with our performance and potential tools and put some actual sales data behind it. We looked at our entire team and assessed what team members could move into roles of supervision and other leadership and the performance levels of the team members (determined by performance review scores).

With that as my starting point, I started to look at the actual sales results and overlaid those with the other information. What I found was striking. Those team members most capable of leadership roles and performing highly typically saw 13-15% growth in their markets.

---

3   *https://www.coachhub.com/app/uploads/2021/12/US_ROI-of-Coaching.pdf*

Those team members who likely couldn't move into supervisory or leadership roles and weren't performing well compared to higher performing peers had <u>negative</u> 8-10% growth rates. I expected to see a difference when we looked at it, but I didn't expect the difference to be so significant.

Sure, I had managers argue with me about how the markets and other factors impacted one employee's performance over another. Yet I continued to restate and return to the team to share that directionally: *We needed to pay attention to what this was saying.* As the HR leader, I knew which of these employees required the most attention and time from our leaders (spoiler alert: the low potential/low performing group), yet we were chasing losses with our attention there.

Our time and, subsequently, our attention is finite, and where we spend it tends to grow. I was getting calls from managers and leaders about the same employees. These employees weren't meeting performance expectations, causing trouble with other team members, and didn't act as though they wanted to be there in the first place.

I wasn't getting calls about the high performers. Actually, let me take that back. The most common time I would receive calls about the high performers was when we needed to put a counteroffer together because it was our last-ditch effort to retain them. Those calls were so frantic that we couldn't afford to lose a person, but since our time and attention were elsewhere, we found ourselves playing defense on our heels. We needed to quickly put together a counteroffer to try and negotiate with that high performer to stay with our organization.

THAT'S THE TRAP! Our high performers, the ones who know the job, understand the expectations, and take the initiative are the team members where our attention would be most valuable. Yet they aren't the ones who tend to draw our attention because they're doing what we want to see them do! Because of this, we focus on the problem areas because our high performers "know what they're doing" and because "they've got it."

When we start working with clients, we assess the current state of their business and HR practices (whether they are formalized or not). We conduct interviews with business stakeholders, including business owners and leaders, managers, supervisors, and key employees. Typically, leaders ask us to talk to their high-performing employees, their managers, and those individuals that the business leaders value and want to make sure their opinions are heard. These are the employees the business would like to keep around. The employees they NEED to keep around.

We ask consistently, *"how do you know you are doing well?"*. Initially, we were surprised by the responses, and we thought it was a fluke. After a while, the responses became almost predictable. Then we realized that it wasn't a fluke. This was a theme. The most common responses we heard sounded like this:

- An awkward chuckle and silence...heh, heh, heh. Well...
- Snarky "well, I haven't been fired yet," or "I'm still here," or
- The uncomfortable and hesitant "um, I don't know" or "no news is good news?"

What?!? Remember, these are typically managers, supervisors, and key employees that business leaders value and want to retain, their high performers! Yet these employees don't know if they are doing well?!? I wish I could say these were outlier responses, but over the last several years, these responses are the most common - by far.

What would YOUR high performers say? Do they know their impact on you, on customers, on team members, and on the organization? Chances are they know some, but they haven't heard the feedback clearly from you. Then, we're caught off-guard when they tell us they received a better offer to join another organization, and we scramble to put something together to try and give them a reason to stay. Never a good position to be in for negotiating.

Here's something you're not going to like hearing from me, but I'll say it anyway. If your business constantly recruits to fill gaps, the issue might be more extensive than just finding great people. Studies have consistently shown that one of the main reasons people leave roles (or choose to leave for little/no pay increase) is often because of their relationship with their leader and how valued they felt in their role. Whether or not an employee feels valued in their position directly correlates to if they know how they are doing.

So, if I take the HR language off for a minute, it sounds like this: **You and your leaders might be the biggest reason you have a recruiting issue. The buck stops here.**

We see this in businesses and with clients today. One business we worked with had north of 80% turnover in its staff when we started. A new leader had come in and was getting integrated into the business. The roles turning over were entry-level, somewhere in the $10-15/hour range. Yes, they had a recruiting issue, but the bigger issue was retaining the employees they had with them.

That leader, James, was adamant about building his supervisors' and managers' leadership and coaching skills and got right to work in doing so. The ship doesn't turn overnight, but it does turn with time and with consistent effort. Where are they now? They aren't satisfied yet, but their turnover is down to 35% in just two years. **What was looking like a recruiting problem was actually a retention problem - their leaders needed leadership and coaching skills.**

Coaching skills. It sounds like a pretty easy, straightforward, and prescriptive response, right? Just coach your team members more effectively! *But of course, why didn't I think to do that before, right?*

I get it. My intent is not to be snarky and make it sound so simple and easy. Coaching takes attention, takes some time, takes some self-reflection, and takes some courage to be *willing* to coach instead of command. In our experiences with leaders, managers, and supervisors, we've seen countless examples of leaders being outstanding in their roles as doers and individual contributors. Because of their success, they are promoted to lead a team. At first the title and the attention are great, and everyone feels good that they got acknowledged and recognized for all of their great work through their promotion to a supervisor.

In far too many instances, though, there is little to no transition or training into an entirely new position. Now they're responsible for getting results THROUGH team members, though we haven't equipped them with HOW to do this.

If you can relate to, or have encountered this yourself, our goal is to meet you where you're at today and equip you with tools you can put into practice immediately. The goal here isn't to make this an overnight success. Instead, the goal is to help you build repeatable behaviors and habits into your everyday practice as you meet with, talk to, and coach your team members. Think of it as a dimmer switch, not a light switch. Are you nudging the dimmer switch brighter every day? That's what we'll be working on here.

Remember the statistic from earlier - where studies have shown that coaching your team members has a more than 570% return on investment? For every minute you spend coaching a team member, that investment will pay off more than 570%[4]. For every minute your leaders and managers spend coaching, that investment will pay off more than 570%. That is exponential.

Yet the reality is this: that same study showed that leaders spent less than 10% of their time coaching team members. Why is that?

If leaders focus on making the time and building the habits to coach, you can increase the amount of time you spend coaching because it

4   *https://www.google.com/url?q=https://www.coachhub.com/app/uploads/2021/12/ US_ROI-of-Coaching.pdf&sa=D&source=docs&ust=1694331049617738&us- g=AOvVaw2vMN0zNaV8isS_si2I1S-h*

will be natural. It's what you do. Then you will be sitting at higher than 10% of your time coaching (remember that statistic, too) and feel the impact in the results your business is achieving.

When we talk to many managers, they say they have a good relationship with their employees. They are frequently checking in with their teams. They talk with them every morning, ask how everything is going, and ask about their families. Yes, those are important, *and* it takes more than this. The type of connections you establish with employees through coaching is more profound than these social conversations. Connecting deeper is what increases engagement, retention, and productivity.

CHAPTER 16

THE PEOPLE SPARK® COACHING MODEL

The coaching model we've been using for the last several years involves three steps: Set it up and LISTEN, Share Feedback, and Solve Together. We will dig into each of these in more detail. This model aims to think about coaching as ongoing conversations and discussions with your team members. It is more than the "How was your weekend? How are the kids?" fly-by discussions you have with your team.

The good news is that we don't use separate models for everyday coaching, recognition, constructive feedback, or progressive discipline - we use the same model and tools. Indeed, the messages are different, but we've found this consistency in the framework helps leaders feel more confident in coaching their team members since we use the same muscles.

COACHING MODEL STEP 1

SET IT UP AND LISTEN: DO NOT PASS GO WITHOUT STARTING HERE

Have you ever had a situation where you felt you had all the information you needed? You felt confident in your position and your message, only to deliver it and find out that there was something you didn't know.

It only takes an example or two in your career to know when you've jumped the gun straight into giving someone feedback. And we have more than two examples we could share, along with the backlash, disengagement, and other negative impacts that came with it.

A few years back, I had a friend who experienced this situation - a manager who jumped the gun. But in this case, my friend was the employee who encountered it. My friends' employer offered summer Fridays where employees could work longer hours Monday through Thursday and leave at noon on Friday. One day my friend got to work an hour late. His boss came to him and said, "You were an hour late today. If it happens again, you will no longer be able to use the summer hours." Period. That was it. No discussion. No questions about what was going on, straight to feedback and consequence. Done!

Here's the thing. The day before, my friend had been diagnosed with cancer. Cancer. It was all he could do to drag himself to work that day. And when he did, chastising was all he heard. Ouch! That changes things. Doesn't it? Not only did this experience have a devastating impact on my friend. It angered and demotivated other employees. That one interaction had a ripple effect on others, and not in a good way.

All the manager needed to do was set it up and listen. Three statements. "Hey. I noticed you were an hour late today. That's not like you. What's going on?" Those three statements would have led to a very different conversation, a very different response, and a very different outcome.

That example is extreme, for sure, yet these things happen daily. Recently we had an employee who did an amazing job researching and identifying a technology solution for one of our clients. I was so excited about the work that was done. As is our tendency, I was prepared to give her great feedback on the work (because, I thought, *OBVIOUSLY*, if she did well, she liked what she was doing), and I was mentally preparing a list of other similar projects where we could use her skills. Yay!

When the moment started, I remembered (thank goodness) to stop and ask her thoughts on it. I said, "The work you did on this project was great - you researched, provided solutions, and did so with humor. It makes me feel like you liked this project. What are your thoughts?"

As it turns out, yes, she did well on the project. Yes, she researched, provided solutions, and added a bit of humor. But you know what? She didn't like it. She shared with me that she could and would do it, but it wasn't her favorite. *Oh.* That information changed things. If I hadn't stopped to ask, I would have moved forward on my assumption that she *did* like it. I would have assigned more work like this with the best intentions of giving her motivating work, only to have her feelings demotivated, doing work she didn't like. While it doesn't mean that she won't be doing work like this in the future, it does mean that when we do, our conversations will be different and not based on my assumptions.

Take the time to set up the discussion and listen. Doing so even works in our personal life to open up conversations. It is a great way to build trust. Recently we were on vacation on a lake with access to a boat and all the fun activities to go with it. My daughter had learned to water ski but was hesitant to try. I kept asking and pushing and telling her to water ski -- this was a chance she had that didn't come around often. She was stubborn, pushed back (not surprising for a 12-year-old), and refused.

When we were alone in the car, I started a conversation. I said, "I noticed that every time there is an opportunity to water ski, you say no and refuse to go. It leads me to believe…." At that point, my daughter jumped in defensively. "No, I don't want to go. It's not a big deal. Stop asking." Then she realized how I started my following sentence, stopped short, and asked, "What does it lead you to believe?" I responded, "It led me to believe that you are scared and afraid of getting hurt." Her defensive wall dropped, and we had a good conversation about her concerns. Yes, that was it.

The conversation also allowed me to clarify my intent using contrasting statements. I said, "It wasn't my intent to push you to water ski. My intent was to make sure you didn't miss an opportunity because this opportunity doesn't present itself very often." We both left the conversation feeling better. The next day, she got on those water skis.

In our rush to check something (like giving feedback) off our list, we bypass the opportunity to ensure we have all our facts and all the information. If you remember the late Paul Harvey (I remember it from listening to WJR out of Detroit in the truck with my dad), his deep, clear voice would tell a captivating story. Then, he would share an angle that caused listeners to become completely perplexed at how this could have happened. His closing line, "the REST of the story," still haunts me. As you meet with your team member, I want you to ask yourself if you have "the REST of the story?"

We miss so much good information and many good opportunities if we don't stop to ask and listen.

Setting it up and listening also gives us a chance to let people know WHY we want to talk with them. Think about it: HR people are used to employees cringing when we ask to meet with them. We aren't taught in school that this is the reaction people must use in the workplace, but we learn it pretty early in our careers. The cringing and shying away happens even when people know nothing is wrong, and not just to HR people, either. Often, employees have this same reaction to managers, too. By taking the time to Set it Up and LISTEN first, we're letting people know <u>why</u> we want to meet with them to put them at ease and limit the cringe.

Okay, but how?

Always ASK. Take a moment and ask a question. Make sure you have all of the information. Make sure you understand the different perspectives and perceptions.

When we start working with a group and training them on the coaching model, we often find managers have the hardest time with the first step, Set it Up and LISTEN. We know what we want to say, and just want to say it. Time is precious. They're ready to jump right in. Let's get to it. This especially happens in situations where a leader has to give constructive feedback. They want to charge in, say their piece, and be finished with the discussion. If you feel that sense of urgency to jump right into feedback, stop and make time to listen.

We first need to let our team members know why we want to talk with them. Are we happy about something they did and want to give them recognition? Did something not go well, and do we need to follow up about it?

The two objectives of Set It Up and Listen are to: 1) let the employee know why we want to meet with them, and 2) ensure we have all the information we need before giving feedback.

The best way we've found to Set it Up and LISTEN is to use the framework from one of our favorite books, Crucial Conversations. This has three components, and you can fill in the blanks as appropriate:

- "I noticed…"
- "It leads me to believe…" or "It makes me feel…."
- "How do you see it?" or "What are your thoughts?"

In the case of my team member, it may sound like:

- "I noticed the last few projects you've completed have gone really well."
- "It makes me feel like you're having fun and enjoying this type of work."

- "How do you see it? What are your thoughts?"

Notice that it's important to ask a question...not just any question. Make sure you ask an open-ended question. Use questions that start with "what" or "how." Be cautious of beginning your question with "do/did" or "could."

Our intent in Set It Up and Listen is to UNDERSTAND. When you ask an open-ended question, beware of some sneaky questions that can send you straight into problem-solving with the employee. While questions like "How can I help you?" or "how can we find a way to..." check the box on being open-ended, the intent of those is to <u>solve</u>. We are too early to solve this as we do not yet understand the whole story and haven't provided our feedback. We'll start solving in Step 3 - Solve Together.

Through this step of the model, expect to have a whole conversation. Your team member will share their thoughts and perspectives, and you will probably have additional follow-up questions to get more clarification on their views and more detailed information. In the conversation with our team member, I asked about her thoughts. I asked what she liked about the project and what frustrated her. I asked what type of work projects she was really jazzed about and what specifically got her excited about them. In the example with my daughter, we had a good conversation about why she was scared and how she felt about the situation in general.

Bottom line - do NOT pass Go into Sharing Feedback until you've finished Set it Up and LISTEN.

COACHING MODEL STEP 1.5

AN INTERMISSION IN REALITY

While we love clear and easy-to-follow models, the reality is that there are (at least) three routes you can take once you've Set it Up and Listened with your employee. It all depends on what you hear and what is uncovered in response to your open-ended question.

- Route 1 - Green Light: Proceed onward into the next step - Sharing Feedback. If you haven't heard new information that would change your feedback direction, move ahead to Step 2.

- Route 2 - Yellow Light: Pause. They've shared new information or other points that change the feedback you were going to share. Move forward with caution by adjusting your feedback based on what you heard or yield if you discover you need more information.

- Route 3 - Red Light: Be there. Show empathy. Sometimes your employee may use the opportunity to share more about what's going on with them, things that are troubling them, or something altogether different. This is where empathy plays an important role. Be there for them. Listen, and ask questions to clarify. Right now may not be the time to trudge forward into feedback. The more important part here is to HEAR them.

If they haven't shared new information, or it doesn't materially change your feedback, then you can proceed to the next step, sharing feedback.

COACHING MODEL STEP 2
SHARE FEEDBACK (IT'S EASIER THAN YOU THINK)

Feedback is about communicating to team members about their work, how their work compares to expectations and why, and what you expect going forward. It's about clarity of expectations. We have not provided effective coaching if we are unclear about our expectations. I know you may not believe me about this, and that's okay. We'll work on that.

Remember the beginning of the book when we talked about the eight factors of engagement? One of the eight is "I clearly understand what is expected of me" (and of course, another is "I know I will be recognized for excellent work."). Sharing feedback ties directly to these two factors of engagement.

In our example, you've started the discussion with your team member and uncovered their perspective and possibly even some new information. You had a good conversation with the sole purpose of understanding, so it's now time to move into sharing your actual feedback.

Your best friend with Sharing Feedback is called BIT, which stands for Behavior - Impact - Tomorrow. It's adapted from the Center for Creative Leadership's Situation-Behavior-Impact (SBI)™ model. I've learned to love and appreciate BIT over the years because the framework helps me take the emotions and the personally charged nature of tough conversations out altogether. BIT keeps us focused on the facts and clear expectations with my team members.

The first element is Behavior. This is where we share the facts of the situation that we know - be it good or needing improvement. What specifically did the employee do? What actions did they take? What did they say? The information you share in Behavior may sound similar to the language you used to Set It Up and Listen (specifically the "what you noticed/saw/heard"). After the conversation with my team member, I moved to Behavior and shared the same specific behaviors -- she researched different options and identified possible solutions. She made it fun with her humor (appropriate humor). There might be some overlap or feeling of redundancy here from Set it Up and LISTEN. That's okay, do it anyway as it provides clarity.

The second element is Impact. This helps answer the questions, "So what?" "Why does it matter?" and "What impact does it have?" We tend to assume our team members know WHY they must do what they do. For recognition, you'll see how amazing this step feels when you share Impact with your team members. This is also a great place to tie back to the values and behaviors you identified earlier. The impact can include how the team member's behavior does or does not align with those values. Also, BIT, especially with constructive feedback, makes the feedback feel less personal and more aligned with the Behavior you need to see corrected.

We worked with a client struggling to get employees reporting to work on time to start the production line. Employees came to work at 8:00 a.m., and the production line didn't begin until 8:15 a.m. The leaders told us that they had been telling employees repeatedly for weeks that they needed to be to work at 7:45 a.m. every day so the production line could start at 8:00 a.m., but the behavior wasn't changing. The leaders were frustrated because this delay of 15 minutes every day (it was also happening after breaks and lunches) was costing the business thousands of dollars a week in lost productivity. It was significant and made a material impact on the business. *Ouch!* We asked, "Have you told them WHY the line needs to start at 8:00?" They hadn't. Employees did not know how much lost productivity occurred in those 15 minutes.

Sure, we may think it's obvious, but as leaders, it is our responsibility to try and understand the purview of our employees, how they perceive the situation. We see 10-15 feet into the fog, while our team only sees 2-3 feet. We must make the expectation as clear as possible. When we do this, they'll better understand why things need to be done a certain way. Once the leader communicated the productivity impact and employees understood it, they saw the desired change.

The final element is Tomorrow. Tomorrow is what you want to see in the future, and it is where the future expectations fit in the feedback. Remember, clarity is vital. With recognition, this gives your team members accolades and reinforces what you want to see them continue doing in the future. It can be as simple as "Thank you.

Keep doing what you are doing." It could also be thinking bigger, "I look forward to seeing how you use this skill in other projects." That feels good, right?!

Constructive feedback clearly buttons up your input with your expectations of what needs to change going forward. It can start with statements like "Going forward, I expect…." or "In the future, it is important that you….".

GREAT NEWS: The framework we use for recognition is the same framework we use for constructive feedback. The reason? Learning to give recognition and include constructive feedback in everyday coaching discussions makes it easier to use when you have those tough conversations with someone.

Let's discuss each of these elements in more detail and share some examples. We'll start first by looking at BIT for recognition. We always recommend starting with recognition because no matter what you do, YOU CAN'T MESS IT UP! And remember the ROI on coaching. Our most significant return on investment is in our high performers, so be sure to start with them first.

RECOGNITION

We get a lot of questions from managers about recognition. Things like "I am not a cheerleader, it's not who I am" or "Why do I have to recognize someone for doing their job? It's what they are paid for."

Notice that nowhere have we mentioned a need for pom poms or cartwheels. This is not about being fake or recognizing behavior for the sake of recognition. This is intentional feedback. What are your employees doing that you want to see repeated [good and valuable performance behaviors]? What are they doing that if they stopped doing it, it would have a negative impact on the business? While recognition can be a feel-good thing, it's about identifying the behaviors you want to continue to see. It reminds team members about the intentional cues that keep them moving in a straight line.

Let's say you have a team member, Betsy. You have been struggling with staffing, can't find employees, and the employees you do have may or may not show up; if they do, they are late. Yet, Betsy is on time every day for her shift, ready to work.

Sure, showing up for her shift is part of what Betsy is expected to do. It's her job, and it's also something you want her to continue doing, especially since you know that staffing has been a challenge. Here's how BIT feedback can sound for Betsy:

> **Behavior**: Betsy, you have been on time for work and stayed for your entire shift for the last month. When you get here, you are ready to jump in and help customers immediately, and you make sure all the work is complete before you leave.

> **Impact**: Your team members have shared with me how much they appreciate the work you do. I know, and your team members know, that when we come to work in the morning, we will be set to work for the day since everything has been taken care of. I know that our customers will receive the service they deserve when you are working.

> **Tomorrow**: Thank you. I appreciate you. I am so glad that you are part of our team.

See? No cheers, no cartwheels, no rhymes.

And think about how you would feel if you were Betsy. Typically, our recognition is "Thank you," "I appreciate your hard work," or "You Rock." With only a few sentences, this BIT feedback increases the impact on our team members. I think Betsy would feel pretty damn good.

Think about some of your most reliable team members. What are they doing every day, and whether it's noticed or not? Take a moment, now, to jot down a few sentences on what your BIT feedback would be for them.

A BONUS CHALLENGE

Thinking through your BIT recognition is one step in the process. Sharing it with your team member is your next step. We often hear leaders share that they feel a little awkward and uncomfortable trying to remember the Behavior-Impact-Tomorrow sequence, and their employee seems awkward in receiving it. That's okay. Keep going!

When you make a choice to share your BIT feedback, I want you to take a few moments to watch and observe. What body language do you see from your employee when you start sharing your BIT recognition? What do you notice in their body language by the end? How do they respond? What do they say?

We build this self-reflection into our coaching program when participants first learn how to share BIT recognition. We frequently find that leaders feel less awkward whenever they have one of these conversations. The responses they see from their team members provide the momentum and encouragement to keep giving recognition. It's the start of the most perfect recognition snowball!

Now let's jump into a constructive feedback example. We will dig in a bit deeper here because it can be trickier.

CONSTRUCTIVE FEEDBACK
BEHAVIOR (CONSTRUCTIVE FEEDBACK)

On the surface, this seems like the easiest part of giving feedback. You're giving the facts and explaining what needs to change. Leaders tend to struggle by not being clear and concise, making it difficult for the employee to know what needs to be done differently. This is especially true when correcting personal behaviors, like attitude and the HOW they are getting their work done.

Let's work through an example. You have a team member, Bob, that has a bad attitude, and it's gotten to a point where you need to meet with him to discuss it. If your feedback about his attitude stays general, it won't be worth anything. In saying he has a bad attitude, you're simply basing your assessment on your assumption of his behaviors, not actually addressing the behavior itself. A bad attitude looks different from one person to the next, and it's subjective. So if we tell someone they have a bad attitude, we will likely get a defensive response. Our goal in Behavior is to get *really* specific about the behavior that needs to change.

What behaviors is he demonstrating that lead you to believe he has a bad attitude? What does a bad attitude consist of? GET SPECIFIC! (Notice a theme here?) Here are a few common examples:

- Rolling their eyes when a suggestion is brought up in a meeting.
- Responding with sarcastic remarks like "been there, done that, not gonna work!"
- Bringing up feedback and suggestions as complaints about other team members.
- Cutting off others in discussion.
- Talking to someone next to them while another team member is talking.

See what these descriptions of bad behavior start to sound like instead? Begin making a list of those behaviors as precisely as you can. Not only does this help you give better feedback to your employee, but it also helps your team member know how others perceive their behavior. It helps prevent back-and-forth arguments between managers and employees if your feedback isn't specific enough.

Once you've gotten *really* specific about Bob's behaviors, your feedback can sound like this:

"Bob, you've rolled your eyes in the last two team meetings when others have brought up suggestions and input. You've also interrupted other team members and cut them off in conversation."

It might sound a little black-and-white, even a little sterile, and that's okay. In Behavior, we're sticking to the facts and getting specific on the behavior we need to see changed. It doesn't have to be long, nor does there need to be drawn-out stories and examples of the Behavior. We're simply stating the facts.

IMPACT (CONSTRUCTIVE FEEDBACK)

Now that we've shared the Behavior with Bob, it's time to share the Impact of this behavior with him. Our Impact statement answers the question "so what?" and helps explain why this behavior is not okay.

The Impact could be many things. In some cases, Impact is the impact of the behavior on the person's performance. It could be the impact on other team members, or it could also be the impact on the business itself. Think through WHY something matters - this is a great place to start coming up with your Impact.

In Bob's case, other team members have started sharing with their leader that they don't want to work with him because they don't feel respected and don't know how he will respond.

Our feedback to Bob for Impact will build on what we shared for Behavior:

> **Behavior**: Bob, you've rolled your eyes in the last two team meetings when others have brought up suggestions and input. You've also interrupted other team members and cut them off in conversation.

> **Impact**: Because of these behaviors, other team members have shared their concerns about working with you. This

behavior also goes against our company values for teamwork and respect. I'm concerned that if this continues, it will impact your performance.

We've now made it clear to Bob WHAT behavior needs to be corrected and shared with him the impact on others and the team. Now we're ready to move on to the final step.

TOMORROW (CONSTRUCTIVE FEEDBACK)

In this final part of sharing feedback, we clarify what we expect of that team member going forward. The Tomorrow statement is where our communication shifts from asking ("do you think you could...?") to telling ("I expect..."). This is where we see leaders hesitate and dilute their feedback by softening it to make them feel more comfortable. The thing is, when we dilute our feedback and the message we need to send to our employees, we aren't being transparent with our expectations - and that isn't kind at all.

In Bob's example, we want him to stop interrupting others and rolling his eyes to others' input in meetings. We also want to **make it clear** that this isn't acceptable behavior and needs to stop. Let's build on the Behavior-Impact we've already put together for Bob, adding Tomorrow here.

> **Behavior:** Bob, you've rolled your eyes in the last two team meetings when others have brought up suggestions and input. You've also interrupted other team members and cut them off in conversation.
>
> **Impact:** Because of these behaviors, other team members have shared their concerns about working with you. This behavior also goes against our company values for teamwork and respect. I'm concerned that if this continues, it will also impact your performance here.
>
> **Tomorrow:** Let me be clear - this is not okay. Going forward,

I expect that you wait for others to finish their statements if you have something you want to contribute to a meeting. The eye-rolling in response to others' suggestions must stop now. If you disagree with others or their approaches, that is okay. I expect you to express that disagreement respectfully and be constructive in helping us get results.

Does it look like a lot of words? Perhaps. You may not need to use as many words. As long as you are specific in your Behavior-Impact-Tomorrow, you will still be delivering clear feedback.

You're getting your point across to Bob in a way that makes it very clear for him to see your expectations for what he needs to do from now on. You're not asking him to "change his attitude." You're telling him specifically to stop eye-rolling and interrupting others - something that is clearly actionable.

CLEAN UP YOUR ROOM.

At times, we hear responses and pushback from frustrated leaders who say, "Shouldn't people already know this?! Why do I have to say this?!"

Ever feel that way?

I used to ask my kids to clean up their rooms, and I'd do things like set a timer and find a prize or reward if they did it well. And every single time, I'd be sorely disappointed in the results. I would go into their rooms and see everything looking *exactly* the same, except for maybe one Lego guy that had been put onto a dresser from the floor.

What happened then? I got frustrated, and I'd repeat myself. I'd raise my voice, saying the same thing over and over: "Clean up your room!"

I don't remember when or where, but I tried something different one day. Instead of my blanket request to "Clean up your room!" I made a list of the specific things that needed to be completed: make the bed, wipe down bathroom counters, pick clothes up off the floor, put them in the laundry chute, etc.

I'm sure you see where I'm going with this story, but do you know what happened that day? Instead of the frustration cycle swirling and repeating, the tasks were *actually* completed. I made it more precise for the kids what they needed to do (all parts of "clean up your room") so they didn't have to try and interpret what I meant. We were able to break the cycle.

While grown-ups are not children, there are some good lessons we'd be remiss to walk past when giving feedback. This is one of them: GET SPECIFIC on what needs to change, why it's essential, and what you expect going forward. The difference this makes - for the employee AND you - is tremendous. Once we get specific and it's clear what the employee needs to do differently, we're ready for the final step.

COACHING MODEL STEP 3

SOLVE TOGETHER

At this point, you've completed Step 1 (Set It Up and LISTEN You were clear to move to Step 2. You've shared feedback using BIT.

The meeting is over, right? No, it's not! Unfortunately, we've seen too many meetings e8nd here, and all the excellent progress gets wiped away because you didn't leave with clarity about where you were going next.

In Solve Together, we get on the same page with our employee so that we all know what will happen. For all of you managers who love to jump straight into "how can I help you?" and "what can I do to support you?" early in the process, this step is for you.

In Solve Together, you'll continue to use open-ended statements and questions. For recognition, we may use this step to get input from the employee on what ideas they have to teach others or share this information with other team members. Examples may sound like:

- What ideas do you have to share this in other departments?

- How can I support you in continuing this?

In constructive feedback, we generally use this step to hear from the employee what their ideas are to correct a situation or behavior. It can also be where we clarify that employees understand what's expected of them. Examples may sound like:

- What is your understanding of the expectations?

- What are you going to do to ensure these expectations are met?

- What do you understand as the next steps for you?

A word of caution here: As the leader, you are not expected to take on the burden or responsibility for your team member changing their behavior. Your role is to provide feedback and expectations and support them with ideas and ways to help them.

Here's what I mean: Let's say you have an employee who hasn't been correctly finishing all of the work by the end of their shift.

You've set it up and listened to them. Nothing new came out of the discussion. You shared BIT feedback with them, "All work isn't being completed at the end of your shift the last two days. It impacts the incoming team members on the next shift by slowing them down from getting the information they need to meet their production goals. This is not okay. Checks must be completed by the end of the shift, and continued failure to do these checks will be considered a performance issue."

In Solve Together, I've seen too many leaders ask, "What can I do to help you complete your work by the end of your shift?" On the surface, the question seems acceptable and even nice. What you are subconsciously doing is taking on the burden instead of addressing the issue of the employee, completing the checks.

Instead, you may ask questions about how you can support your employee. Here are some suggestions for how you can Solve Together without taking the burden on your shoulders. Some of our go-to questions for Solve Together in constructive feedback sound like this:

- What ideas do you have to be able to meet this requirement?
- What have you considered or tried already?
- What plans do you have to correct this?

Okay, so we've gone through constructive feedback (don't worry, we'll go through it some more). Those discussions aren't the only ones where the coaching model and BIT feedback can impact. Remember the quote we shared earlier, "culture isn't what you say; it's what you allow."

When you think about the culture you're reinforcing, what behaviors do you want to recognize and want to continue? What behaviors are you choosing to allow that break down the culture you want?

Coaching: It's not just the bad and the good. It's also everything in between.

The coaching model isn't just for recognizing strong performance or correcting behavior that is out of bounds. These tools are even more powerful when you use them to support and engage your teams in the day-to-day.

Think about a situation where a team member has been asked to do something differently. Perhaps you've asked them to try a new system, use a new script, analyze data differently, or execute a unique new process. Now that you've asked them to try something new, they are starting at the beginning of the change curve.

Remember way back when we talked about change? As people move from Frustration/Depression into Experiment (on the Kübler-Ross model), those are CRITICAL moments to engage your team members in a coaching conversation.

They're taking the first steps, and while they may not be perfect, they are trying on the new change. They haven't necessarily bought in yet. They may be at Experiment, not yet moving into Decision or Integration.

NOTE: These everyday situations, when team members are trying new tasks and behaviors that warrant recognition, don't always catch our attention. They don't come with warning lights to tell us that this is an excellent time to recognize our team members. Often, these are disguised as typical, nondescript actions with a team member "just" doing their job. This is partly why it can be difficult for leaders to take the time in the moment to make the connection with their team members. These actions don't require us to step in and coach a team member with something they're doing wrong. Instead, we're looking for something different - catching our team members doing what needs to be done.

One client who worked through a merger used this skill daily. While this was a merger of two organizations, the business used the opportunity to realign its structures and implement new systems, creating a space where everyone was on the same page. There were many opportunities to coach, encourage, recognize and support. There was a definite period in their change when many of their team members were frustrated and depressed. The comments they would hear regularly were, "why do we have to do this?", "I am never going to figure this out," "this is so complicated," and then when in depression, there was more silence.

Their HR Manager, who knew many of the employees well, would talk to and coach individual employees. He would check-in when he walked through their locations and noticed that typically verbal team members were quiet.

"Last week, you shared concerns about the new system when I was here. Today I haven't heard you say anything. In fact, you walked away when I arrived. It makes me feel like you are more frustrated than you have been. How are you feeling?" Through these conversations, the HR Manager heard concerns he had not heard before. He provided feedback to employees on appropriate and inappropriate ways to share their concerns and feedback.

Most importantly, he was able to show he cared. Employees felt valued. They felt they were heard, asked for their thoughts, and their leaders cared about them. It was an exciting day when the leaders heard more feedback indicating that employees were moving into acceptance and adoption. The CEO shared that he heard employees say things like, "I didn't know how to do this in the new system, so I did some research online."

Hallelujah! The CEO also took this opportunity to coach the behavior he wanted to see continue. "You just shared that you researched a process for the new system. It makes me feel like things are improving, and you are identifying resources. How are you feeling?" In this case, the BIT feedback to the employee was definitely recognition, as this was exactly the behavior the CEO hoped to see. The CEO shared with the employee that researching solutions to the issues she was facing would help her and the business be more successful and that they would be able to support their customers faster than they had been. After giving the feedback, he also asked her thoughts on how to share this information with other team members (to encourage others along the curve as well).

We've talked about the situations in which you can use the coaching model and tools, now let's actually apply it.

We'll start with focusing on using the coaching model for recognition. There are two reasons. First, recognition is more powerful and has a better return on investment. According to Buckingham and Goodall in *Nine Lies About Work*, "Negative feedback is 40 times more effective as a team leadership approach than ignoring people. **Positive attention is 30 times more**

powerful than negative attention in creating high performance on a team." Wow.

Second, YOU CANNOT MESS IT UP! Even if you don't get all the words right, even if it doesn't flow the way you want it to, and even if it feels clunky to work through at first, you are still giving recognition that is multiple times more powerful and meaningful than a "good job" and pat on the back. These are the types of everyday situations that, if we choose to stop and acknowledge and recognize them, will start to make a significant impact on the culture of your business.

PUT IT ALL TOGETHER - Write out your talking points.

On paper, put down the actual words you want to leave your mouth as you give your recognition. We've broken it down for you here so you can build your script.

Coaching Step	Conversation Prompts	YOUR Words! Using these prompts, write out the words you want to say in your situation.
Set it Up & LISTEN	I noticed / I saw / I heard... It leads me to believe / It makes me feel... What are your thoughts? Or how do you see it?	

Share Feedback: BIT	**Behavior.** What behavior/action do you want to recognize? Get specific? Get granular so they know what to REPEAT.	
	Impact. What's the impact of the behavior on their work, you, teammates, the business, etc.? Why does it matter?	
	Tomorrow. What do you want to see tomorrow? Thank them, encourage them.	
Solve Together	Use open-ended questions here to engage them.	
	How can you learn from their work and pass it on to others?	
	What ideas do you have to continue this?	

TAKE ACTION - GO AND DELIVER THE RECOGNITION!

Once you've worked through the worksheet and planned the talking points for your recognition, your job isn't over yet. Now it's time to take action. DELIVER the recognition by going through Set it up, LISTEN, Share Feedback, and Solve Together with your team member!

133

Does it feel a little clunky at first? Probably. It might even feel a little awkward. Some participants have shared that it took a few times for them to feel more comfortable using the framework.

Will your employee be a little hesitant at first to engage in the discussion? Maybe. We often don't realize how frequently our interactions are around problems or situations that need to be corrected. Team members have the "being sent to the principal's office" feeling when we say we want to talk with them. I know I've felt that way, and I'm sure you have too.

DO IT ANYWAY. We did this with a client a while back and asked them how it went. More than delivering the feedback, we wanted them to pay attention to what happened in the interaction. What did they notice happened in the discussion? How did their team member respond? Some of their responses were even better than we expected:

- "I felt confident in providing positive recognition. It felt like a culture-setting conversation."

- "This team member is often negative in general. This conversation started with a negative tone here, too, because I hadn't been to his work area yet. His attitude improved when I told him some of the things I was working on since we last talked, and even more so when I encouraged him to share his ideas with me."

- "This person has always been positive, and seemed surprised to be getting good feedback on what she considered was expected of her."

- "It felt a little unusual going into the conversation of delivering this specific dialogue. During and afterwards, though, it became clear how this is so effective at building a relationship of trust between coworkers."

YES! That's what we want!

REFLECTION TIME.

Now that you've also taken the time to write out your talking points AND deliver your feedback to your team member, I want you to take a moment to reflect, too.

- How did your team member respond? What happened?
- What did they say? How did they engage?
- How did you feel about delivering the feedback? What felt easier than expected? What was more challenging than you expected?

CHAPTER 17

COACH TO MANAGE PERFORMANCE

In many cases, people connect coaching with providing performance feedback. Yes, coaching and giving feedback are crucial aspects of managing performance. While there are spots where they overlap or are similar, there are some key distinctions. As a result, we look at them separately. Coaching is an everyday, ongoing process—not a one-time event. In too many cases, unfortunately, people view managing performance as an event and a process to be completed - often because it happens so infrequently.

Of course, processes are important, and forms can be important – but processes and forms are not the be all to end all. Processes and forms can SUPPORT your overall goals, but they shouldn't BE the goal. So, as we talk about managing performance, we will talk about processes and forms–but they will be discussed in terms of the goals and culture of the business. The processes and forms are expected to support the behaviors of your culture you identified in Chapter 2.

We will also discuss managing performance in terms of providing feedback to employees (everyday recognition and constructive feedback), as part of a more formal, structured review process, and then separately discuss addressing performance issues. In these instances, we'll talk about holding employees accountable when the everyday coaching hasn't been effective at changing behavior, and the behavior has now turned into a pattern.

PERFORMANCE REVIEW PROCESSES

I have to admit, I cringe when people ask specifically about performance reviews or a performance management process and whether they should have one. I cringe because the focus tends to be on the process itself, not the outcome. The focus is on checking a box and completing a form. A business owner at a speaking engagement asked us, "How often do I have to have performance reviews with my employees? Once a year? One every six months, once a quarter?" This is a focus on a process, not on the act of giving coaching or feedback itself.

Rather than focusing on the process, the focus should be on <u>giving clear feedback</u>. The goal of performance management is that a leader and employee have the same understanding of the employee's performance compared to identified standards.

What does this mean?

- Are the standards used to assess performance the same standards the employee understands?
- Does the employee walk away from the conversation with the same understanding of their performance as the manager?
- Do team members know how they are doing? (Does that question sound familiar? It should.)

Remember earlier when we discussed our assessment process, and that the common theme we hear when asking, "how do you know you are doing well?" The theme has been the same, now several years and counting. Businesses sometimes have performance review processes, and in some cases, they don't. One thing to notice is that even those that *do* have a process are still giving us the same answers. That means that the process is not effective. The employees' understanding of their performance against standards is *not* clear. It's a process for the sake of process and is not achieving its intended goals because the BEHAVIOR of coaching and giving feedback isn't effective.

So, the answer to the first question is really another question, specific to each business and each organization: How often do you need to connect with managers, supervisors, and employees for them to know they are doing well? More importantly, how do you need to structure the conversation, so everyone truly knows? That's not just about a process; it's about the conversation.

The more frequently you have coaching conversations with your employees, the easier performance review conversations will be. Then it's no longer about the content of the review, it's now about summarizing the discussions you have already been having.

Build the Process to Follow the Coaching Model

The coaching model has the steps needed to have an effective performance conversation. Use those steps to create your process. Step 1 is Set It Up and LISTEN, where your goal is to understand the team member's thoughts and perspectives. If this is our starting point, use a strategy that will encourage you and your managers to understand before jumping right into feedback.

- Give team members notice that you will be having a performance conversation. Allow them time to reflect on their performance compared to the standards, expectations, and behaviors.
- Have team members complete an initial self-review with their perspectives (here, a form's purpose is to provide some support and structure for team members to give their thoughts and make it easier for them).
- Start the conversation with Set It Up and LISTEN. "Our goal today is to talk about your performance over the past few months. How do you think it has been going since our last conversation?"

Once you and your team member have had a chance to talk through their perspectives and you have asked good clarifying questions, you can move to Step 2 and share feedback using BIT. You can actually write your feedback on your performance form in the BIT format, making it easier for you and much clearer for your team members.

Finally, you can close the conversation with Step 3 of Solve Together. You can ask questions like "how would you summarize our conversation today?" or "what ideas do you have to continue to use your strengths in the next few months?"

TIE THE PERFORMANCE PROCESS TO VALUES AND GOALS

Remember that the goal of performance management is that you and your team member have the same understanding of their team member's performance compared to identified standards. With this being the case, you need to ensure you have identified the standards. No need to panic; you did this earlier. It's the values and behaviors you identified to build your intentional culture. Those are the behavior standards. Your productivity standards are the goals and key performance indicators you also identified earlier. Those aspects, values, behaviors, and goals are the north star to which all energy and processes should be focused. See how we're using the process to reinforce the goals and behaviors you intend for your business?

In Set It Up and LISTEN, ask your team member how they feel they have demonstrated the behaviors of each of the values. Ask for specific examples. Ground yourselves on the goals of the team member's role and ask the team member how they have performed against those goals. Then you can provide feedback, using BIT, on examples you have seen when they have demonstrated the behaviors (or not). Stay on the path to the north star.

CHAPTER 18

COACH TO ADDRESS PERFORMANCE CONCERNS

We coach employees to change their behaviors or performance to meet expectations and follow the framework we described to help make changes more successfully. We also recognize there are cases where it doesn't happen. In some instances, behaviors become a pattern. You find that you have coached, made your expectations clear, and ensured the employee understands your expectations. You provided support and resources to the employee.

But...

The behaviors aren't changing. They still don't show up to work on time, aren't meeting deadlines, and are still demonstrating a poor attitude that negatively impacts the morale of the rest of the team. Whatever it may be, it's not changing.

In previous chapters, we introduced the coaching and BIT models for sharing feedback. We will build on these concepts by discussing constructive feedback and progressive discipline.

Here's what tends to happen. A manager coaches, and coaches, and coaches (feels a bit like a broken record), and each time they talk to the employee, there is more frustration and intensity. The problem is that the manager feels the increased frustration but doesn't typically share it with the employee. The employee doesn't pick up on it, and it feels like a normal conversation to them. Well, until one day, the manager says, "That's it! I'm done!" The team member is either put on a final warning or terminated. The employee is left confused and wondering, *What just happened?!?* The manager is left feeling, *Geez, how did you not see this?!?*

As we said earlier, the goal of performance management is to ensure that the manager and employee have the same understanding of performance against identified standards. It is also vital that the employee and manager understand where the employee stands as it relates to progressive discipline. In the example we described above, the seriousness of the situation progressively elevated in the manager's mind. Yet, in the employees' mind, they were having ongoing conversations and not much more. It's essential to ensure that the employee understands the seriousness and that it is getting progressively worse.

As behaviors become patterns that are not corrected, we start progressive discipline. Typically, a progressive discipline process includes actions like a verbal warning, a written warning, suspension, or a final warning. Each business may follow a different approach, and this information (at least in general) is included in their employee handbook. However, you can follow a progressive discipline process by building on BIT and adding another I.

We like to call it **BITI2**. Behavior (B), Impact (I), Tomorrow (T) and [a second] Impact (I2). Let's go through this in detail.

- **Behavior**: How you describe the behavior is not likely to change from your previous conversations. You should describe the specific behavior the employee is exhibiting in the same level of detail. As the seriousness increases (because behaviors are not changing), you will want to add a few new pieces of information. Since you previously discussed these

142

situations with the employee, you will add the times you discussed them. "We have talked about this three times in the last two weeks" or "this is the second time we have talked about this behavior." Then add that it is becoming a pattern of behavior. "This is a pattern. This is not okay." Do you see how those two things indicate that the conversation has increased in its seriousness?

- **Impact**: The impact should remain the same as in your previous coaching conversations. You will use similar language as you used previously.

- **Tomorrow**: Tomorrow should also remain the same since your expectations should be the same as they have been, clarifying what you expect to see changed by the employee.

- **Impact 2**: This is the most significant change in your conversation. The second impact is the impact on the employee if they fail to make the necessary changes in behavior or the impact on the employee if they continue not to meet expectations.

Progressive discipline using BITI2 could sound like this (we will use Bob from our previous example).

- **Behavior:** Bob, in our last meeting, you rolled your eyes when others were talking, and you cut off other team members when they shared their thoughts. This is the third time we have discussed my concerns about your behavior in meetings, which is not okay.

- **Impact:** Because of this, other team members have shared their concerns about working with you and they don't feel respected.

- **Tomorrow:** I expect that if you have something you want to contribute, you bring it up in a way that doesn't interrupt others. I also expect the eye-rolling to stop immediately.

- **Impact 2:** If you continue to demonstrate these behaviors in our meetings, you will receive a written warning.

In this case, we have increased the seriousness by sharing what will happen if this behavior continues. If you have had this conversation and it continues, the second impact will continue to increase in seriousness. For example:

- If you continue to behave in this way, it will result in further disciplinary action, up to and including termination.

- If you continue to behave in this way, you will receive a final written warning.

- Continued failure to meet these expectations will result in the termination of your employment.

We work with many managers who are hesitant to make these statements. Leaders don't want to be harsh or mean; they want to be nice.

Let's talk about what it means to be nice. Have you ever heard the term "Minnesota-nice"? I was born and raised in Minnesota, so we consistently hear the phrase. On the surface, it feels like a good thing that people are "so nice in Minnesota." It often reminds me of the quote from Thumper in the movie *Bambi*, when he says, "if you can't say something nice, don't say anything at all." It results in many things that need to be told but are left unsaid. In this case, it's <u>not</u> nice because you are not sharing important information the other person needs to know.

Rather than worrying about whether or not we are being *nice*, let's focus on being *kind*, which means that you say what needs to be said, in a respectful and caring way. Being kind is being empathetic and demonstrating high courage and consideration.

If this sounds like you, where you feel like adding the second Impact could come across as threatening to your team member, go back to one of the earlier tools we discussed, contrasting statements. This can be how you can share the second Impact with your employee. It may sound like this: "My intent is not to make you feel threatened or scared. My intent is to be very clear so you understand what may happen if this pattern of behavior isn't corrected."

Over the last 20+ years, I have had many leaders ask for assistance in this process. They want help saying things the best way (which we already addressed in the coaching model and BIT). They also want assistance in putting these conversations in writing, specifically with written warnings. Many leaders coach employees well and then sit down in front of the computer and struggle with what to type. There's no need to struggle because you already have the framework. Write the written warning in the BITI2 format, and you will have a thorough and clear written warning. Yes, that's right, BIT and BITI2 can translate to the written form as well.

SOMETIMES IT DOESN'T WORK OUT

There are times when, despite all of your very best effort, a team member isn't making the changes you need to see them succeed. Sometimes in larger organizations, this might be the time where the underperforming team member is placed on a pretty rigorous 60- or 90-day performance improvement plan where they are expected to meet a list of criteria to keep their job.

For many reasons, I've seen both managers and employees view the performance improvement plan (the PIP) as the kiss of death. The *"I know you aren't going to make it, but I have to give you this final warning to cover my butt if we end up terminating you."* How incredibly un-inspiring is that message or that reaction to the tool? Certainly when the tool's name describes *improving performance.*

Remember what we said was the primary purpose of performance management? We want to ensure the employee and the manager have the <u>same</u> understanding of the performance and expectations. If we use this as our intent, having these discussions when nothing else seems to be working can be so much easier.

THE POWER OF CHOICE

Over the last several years, as I've coached leaders, I've come to *really* appreciate an honest heart-to-heart with the employee. If you are starting to consider termination, or if you're also considering some kind of "last chance" performance improvement plan, then I strongly encourage you to have what I call "the end of the road conversation."

In these discussions, the manager meets with the employee to share where they are overall. Too often, employees don't know that things are "that serious" until they hear there is potential to lose their job. This meeting is intended to let them know that there are two routes here at the end of the road, staying and working through a performance improvement plan successfully or evaluating if this is the time to look at options outside of your organization. Here's how it sounds:

- *Over the last several months, I've been sharing the same feedback that key objectives in your role are not being met today. I have shared with you that I expect that you consistently make ten sales calls weekly to new prospects, and to date, that has not happened.*

- *I want to let you know where we are in this process. My intent is not to send the message that I don't think you can improve; my intent is to be clear with these expectations and allow you the opportunity to see what option is best for you.* (Notice the contrasting statements).

- *Your performance needs to be immediately improved, and that improvement must be sustained. To help you with that, we can put together a rigorous performance improvement plan with objectives for you to meet over the next 90-days to continue your employment. The plan itself is not a guarantee of employment for that time. (This is Choice #1)*

- *This plan will not be easy, and your progress must be sustained. You are responsible for your performance and meeting these expectations. I will support you but you need to own it.*

- *I also want you to think about and consider whether this is where you want to be right now. If you choose that you'd instead use this time to transition out of the organization, we can work together on what that transition would look like. (This is Choice #2)*

- *I realize this is a lot to think about and that it is a big decision. Let's plan to get back together on Monday to talk more about what route you would like to take.*

What's amazing is that giving team members a choice and the *dignity* to make that choice for themselves demonstrates your values and can mitigate a lot of your risk. Your team member who decides they are 100% in on a performance improvement plan has stronger momentum heading into the PIP to make changes happen—and for performance changes to stick. For the team member who decides it's the right time to leave, you get the benefit of having some time to work with them on that transition and make it a great outcome for them.

I've had instances where employees are grateful for the choice and knew for a long time that the role wasn't something they wanted to continue. They needed the opportunity to make this choice for themselves. There's so much power in this discussion with your team member, for you and them. Don't let this opportunity to connect with them pass you by.

PERFORMANCE IMPROVEMENT PLANS

Say our employee considers both options and chooses to take the performance improvement plan. By making this choice on their own, they may be more committed to it than they otherwise might be.

Are performance improvement plans helpful? They absolutely can be, but it truly depends. The fact that they're called "performance IMPROVEMENT plans" signals that they're intended to IMPROVE performance. As you approach a performance improvement plan with an employee, there are some critical things to consider, so let's break it down.

- **Performance has to improve and remain there.** The main message for your team member should be that the employee's performance must be immediately improved AND sustained. While you're working through a performance improvement plan in this instance, a dip in performance after this PIP does not guarantee that the employee will get another chance.

- **Get specific and measurable where you can.** What specific goals need to be accomplished for the next 60 or 90 days to get the employee back on track? Here's a watch out! I often see managers wanting to put ALL the things the employee is behind on [for the entire year] into their 60 or 90-day plan. AVOID THIS! Your best bet here is to consider what would put that employee on the right trajectory that, if they continue to perform in that way, would lead them closer to their annual goals and objectives.?

- **Be reasonable!** This goes along with the last piece of advice. Do not ask your underperforming employee to meet a year's worth of performance in 60 days. Nope. What is REASONABLE that will put them on track if they do?

- **Be ready.** Performance improvement plans do NOT mean handing your team member a document, wishing them well, and moving on your merry way. Meet with your employee at least once a week for the duration of the performance improvement plan. You will constantly be asking them (as part of your Set it Up and LISTEN), "What progress have you made on your plan since our last meeting?" The coaching doesn't end just because you've entered the PIP phase, in fact it's even more important now. Be prepared with clear BIT feedback on what is working, what isn't working, what's going well, and what isn't.

- **Just because you intend for the plan to be a 60 or 90-day plan does not mean you're required to complete the entire time if performance isn't improving.** That's why it is so crucial for you to ask about their performance every week in your update with them, and why it is crucial that you give feedback as well. If performance improvement is *not* progressing weekly, you may consider ending the PIP early and terminating employment at that time. That is okay. You'll want to be sure that your PIP documentation has a phrase or statement that says that the PIP is not a guarantee of employment throughout the PIP. If you feel your team member is not making progress, this is a great time to use Set It Up and Listen. "We started the PIP a month ago. In the first two weeks, you made progress. In the last three weeks, you have not made any progress at all. It makes me feel like this is not a priority for you. How do you see it?"

We mentioned earlier that where you focus is what grows. We just covered the areas around performance, progressive discipline, and performance improvement plans. Those things are essential and areas in which leaders and managers have many questions -- but we don't want to spend all our time as leaders here. We want to continue focusing on the areas with the most ROI -- recognition, engagement, and retention.

CHAPTER 19

WHAT IS ENGAGEMENT?

Why does engagement matter? Isn't it just a buzzword business owners like to throw around? There are a couple of answers to that.

Is it a buzzword? Yes.

Does it have some impressive data behind it? Also, yes.

A 2017 Gallup study titled *State of the American Workplace* showed that higher employee engagement leads to fewer safety incidents, fewer quality defects, improved employee attendance, and improved customer satisfaction, among many other factors. Here are a few:

- 41% lower absenteeism
- 24% lower turnover
- 28% less shrink (depending on the industry, also known as scrap)
- 70% fewer employee safety incidents
- 17% higher productivity
- 21% increased profitability.

Yes, having an entire workforce of engaged employees would be wonderful. An engaged employee is 17% more productive than a disengaged employee. It might not sound like much, but over time, that means that your engaged employee can accomplish six days of work in a five-day workweek. What would it look like if you had a couple more employees who were engaged? What if instead of having 33% of your team engaged, you had 45%? Or 60%? What could your team accomplish? What could your business achieve?

These behaviors, repeated over time, will shift your culture from one that happens **to** you to one that is intentionally built. Recognition also plays a key role in engaging and retaining the great employees you have in your organization. Why? Think about it. Pay can always be adjusted, and the business across the street can do that. We can always add some new or weird perk or benefit to our list of things we offer for our employees—the business next door can do that, too.

The thing that can't be replicated? Strong relationships that are built on trust, where team members get recognized for their work (I didn't say it was pay-related, just that good work was recognized). As a recruiter, I loved recruiting for talent against other companies that I knew didn't offer the same relationships that mine could. Give me those companies to recruit for any day of the week - it wasn't even fair.

As we shift our focus on engagement, I want you to understand that several levers can help build a strong culture that engages and retains employees. Compensation plays a role, but it isn't the only one. We'll come back to that in a bit.

No doubt you've heard something about "engaged" or "disengaged" employees if you've read any business headlines or articles in the last few years. There are headlines about how many employees are disengaged and how few are engaged.

Let's break down engagement a little bit before we dig into what we can do about it.

Engaged employees are your team members who are there every day, your go-to's when it comes to ideas and finding ways to improve processes, systems, or the business overall. These team members are the ones we'd love to clone (or at least copy and paste) because we know that when we give them a project to complete, it will be done and done well.

Disengaged employees are slightly harder to describe. These employees are *fine*. They're there, and you can count on them most of the time. They may fly a little below the radar, so they're never underperforming, but it seems like they never go even an inch beyond what's expected. They do their job, get a paycheck, and go home.

Actively Disengaged employees are those team members who may be stirring things up. They are disengaged, and they are taking action. They might be loud with their resistance and feedback to any changes or anything they ask. They might be actively looking for and applying for other roles while still working (in your business). They're the pot-stirrers, and most items in the rumor mill have gone through them at least a time or two.

The same study from Gallup showed about 33% of employees in the United States are engaged in their roles. This study showed that about 16% of employees are actively disengaged, and 51% of American workers are disengaged. Soak on that for a moment as you think about your team. Similar studies are completed frequently without much fluctuation. Some studies indicate that the percentage of engaged employees may be closer to 36% and actively disengaged employees as low as 14%.

Either way, only about a third of your employees are engaged.

I think about Engaged | Disengaged | Actively Disengaged on a continuum. One person may be disengaged but occasionally has some bright spots that show they can shift into that engaged space. Like the change models we talked about earlier, our team members' location on this engagement continuum is fluid, and it shifts throughout the year and seasons of their careers.

Think about the continuum above related to your team members today:

Actually   Disengaged   Engaged
Disengaged

- Where are they on this continuum?
- What leads you to believe that?
- What signs/symptoms/examples come to mind making you think this?

I like to look at this as a continuum because it allows our team members' engagement to be more fluid, just as it is in ordinary life. There are seasons when we all are highly engaged in what we are doing and are "in the flow." There are also seasons where we drift away from that a bit more. Our goal is to keep our team members engaged and notice when they may be in a less-engaged season.

Where you place team members on this continuum is not right or wrong, good, or bad; it's a data point. It helps us determine where team members are and, as a result, what we can do to increase their engagement (move them to the right).

We see many leaders and managers get excited to put team members on the far right of the continuum, like, "Yay! I am good! Look at how many of my team members are engaged!". Yes, it's great AND more engagement doesn't mean you have arrived. You're not done (it's not a static place, remember?). Remember where we get the best ROI? It's with our engaged employees, high performers, and rock stars. So, we need to focus our time there. These are your rock stars, the ones taking the initiative. They are two steps ahead of everyone else -- so to keep them engaged, you need to be two steps ahead of the team members who are already two steps ahead. It takes time, it takes thought, and it takes intention.

Disengaged employees tend to fall just below the radar and not catch our eyes as leaders because they seem fine. *Fine* doesn't achieve our business goals, and it doesn't provide excellent service to our customers. This is typically the most significant portion of your population, and there are a few key actions you can take to make a heck of a difference in their engagement.

Then we have our actively disengaged employees. As I reflect on team members that I've worked with over the years who have actively disengaged, the common thread across them is their passion. They were fired up, though it may not be directed in a terribly constructive way. In my experience, these actively disengaged employees were, at one point, engaged team members, until something happened. Too often, I've heard from these employees that they brought up ideas and suggestions and offered feedback in the past. Their ideas and feedback continued to go unheard and unacknowledged by their leaders. Nothing was done with their feedback, and there was no follow-up. That passion was there when they were more constructively engaged, but without being nurtured, it turned into active disengagement.

While I'm not suggesting that every actively disengaged employee can be turned and become engaged, many people find that it's often easier to get movement from those with passion (even like actively disengaged) than those who are more apathetic (disengaged). Bottom line? Don't write off your actively disengaged employees as a pain in the side. Their behavior might not be okay now, and we can still use tools like coaching and other engagement ideas to improve it.

One final thought on engagement and determining where your team members might be on that continuum. Each of us have differing levels of engagement throughout our careers. We have roles or times in our personal lives where we are very much engaged. We have points in time where we are closer to the middle of disengaged, where our passion in our work isn't as strong as it was before. The point isn't to rate where someone is today and classify them in that way forever. It's to use this as a place to connect with them through your coaching and using your coaching as a way to engage them more fully.

CHAPTER 20

THE FACTORS OF ENGAGEMENT

There is so much information about engagement today: books, articles, podcasts, checklists, and surveys. It can be overwhelming. It feels like a long exhaustive list of activities, and then you must decide which ones to try. Dartboard? Draw out of a hat? What?!? You will find that the thing that impacts engagement the most is the skill we have already discussed: Coaching.

Engagement Through Coaching and Attention: When things make you go "hmmm. . ."

Think about the continuum activity you just completed and the signs, symptoms, and examples that helped determine where your team members are today on it.

- Has Susan recently seemed quieter than usual? Notice that she has not jumped into a new project with the excitement she used to exhibit.

- Does Sam seem like he's *really* perked up recently on this new assignment? Has he surprised you with some of his work quality (in a good way!)?

Thinking about and observing your team can help unearth the little nuances that will help you better engage with them. Let's take Susan's example and apply the coaching model.

SET IT UP AND LISTEN:

You: Susan, I noticed you've been a little quieter than usual, and it looks like your reaction to new projects recently is different than it's been in the past. What's up?

Susan: Yeah, I've felt a little off recently for sure. I've been pretty excited about the work we've done recently, but it seems like we're onto the next thing once it's finished. It makes me feel like I'm just a machine, chugging along.

You: Oh wow, Susan. Thank you for sharing. I had no idea you felt that way, and I appreciate you being honest about it. My intent is not to make you feel like you're a machine, just here to get work done. My intent is to make you feel like you're a part of a great team that supports one another, and where your work and effort are valued and appreciated.

Susan: Thanks, I mean, I don't know how to make it better, but that's where I'm at today.

SHARE FEEDBACK:

You (**Behavior**): Susan, you always speak up and ask questions, and I've always seen you face challenges with a little fun and competition.

You (**Impact**): When you do this, you set the tone for others on the team, and I love the role modeling you do in these things. You think about challenges in a very creative way, and because of that, you've cracked things that have taken others so much longer to accomplish.

You (**Tomorrow**): I appreciate you. I appreciate having you on our team and seeing all you teach others just by being yourself.

Susan: Oh, wow. Thank you. I didn't know that it had an impact on other people.

SOLVE TOGETHER:

You: Yes! And I appreciate you speaking up right now to let me know what was on your mind. I don't want you to feel like that and I am interested in talking about how we can make sure you feel supported and valued. I'd love to hear some of your thoughts on ways we can make it not feel like it's finishing one thing and moving on to the next.

Susan: Well, I've thought a little about that. I don't think it needs to be much but having some way to celebrate and acknowledge our results as we close out one project and move on to the next could be a way to build momentum....

We were training with a client, working with supervisors to notice these moments, to step into a coaching conversation, to ultimately increase engagement. During the training, we had the supervisors practice (aka role play), with pairs taking turns role-playing the supervisors and the employee. They had to practice noticing and speaking to what they saw their "employee" do, with examples like shrugging their shoulders, hanging their head, looking excited, rolling their eyes, and others. They were only practicing Step 1 of the Coaching Model, Set it Up and Listen, not even going all the way through it.

When we were finished, we asked those playing the employee role how they felt. We got reactions like "I felt valued" and "I felt like someone cared enough about me to notice." They were saying this with sincerity, even though this was a role-playing activity. If it can have that impact during a role play, what impact do you think it would have on your team members? That attention will increase engagement; the business across the street cannot replicate that.

> *"The greatest gift you can give another is the purity of your attention." ~ Richard Moss*

Here's the thing: Often, we fear what our employees might say if we ask them what is going on, so we take the road not to say anything at all. Using what we see through those observations and facts can help us understand what our employee is going through in those moments. Remember, our goal is to keep moving them towards engagement on the continuum. Paying attention to them, noticing where things might seem a little off, and, more importantly, ASKING about them are all ways to begin to make that movement happen. You already have the tools to do these things. Now, it's time to put them into practice.

We mentioned before that sometimes we miss the stuff right in front of us, like the opportunities to recognize employees. So, when do you think leaders typically realize they need to focus on retaining their high performers? When they have turned in their resignation. I remember constantly feeling awkward having "retention" discussions with team members after they notified us that they were leaving. It was always too late! By observing and understanding where your team is *today*, you can more easily step into coaching conversations using this information to a point where you can significantly impact your team members and their overall engagement.

Building engagement with your team happens in the realness of these everyday interactions - where you notice and give attention to your team members.

Is there a drawback to engagement? Possibly, depending on how you look at it. Engaged employees may take more time to coach, to connect them to how their work impacts the business, and to continue having developmental discussions. These often feel like "extra" and "nice-to-haves." Yet, our most engaged employees are the ones who crave these the most. As leaders, we often feel that when someone is fully functioning and engaged, "they've got it, they're good." As a result, we leave them off on a proverbial island by themselves without coaching or feedback.

Engaging your employees means connecting and developing them, where you're working to stay a step ahead. It means going further than giving the directions to just "do this" and instead taking the time to explain the why, impact, and importance. Suppose the path to seeing more productivity, fewer attendance issues, improved performance, and customer service involved investing your time in growing these team members. **Would you be willing to make the investment?**

Think about it as a financial investment. Where is most of your time spent coaching team members today? If you're like most leaders, you get distracted by what ISN'T happening and are spending your time managing and correcting the issues or trying to nudge others along to meet the acceptable levels of performance.

At best, you're likely breaking even. If you're putting your own \$20/hour investment into these discussions, you may only be getting \$20/hour or less in return. When that's my money, I start to see some issues with that.

What about your engaged employees? What does your return look like if you're spending your time with them, connecting the dots, helping them grow and develop, and helping them take on more and more in the business? That \$20/hour investment may earn back \$22/hour or more. When that's my money, I like how that investment pays off.

Look at your continuum again - your engaged, disengaged, actively disengaged employees. With what team members do you spend the majority of your coaching time? What value and impact do you see as a result of your investment?

Engagement does more than help your business increase productivity and decrease absenteeism. Engagement also makes work easier, fun, and less drama filled. When teams are under stress, particularly when you're short-staffed, your attention gets pulled away from the team members who are there and away from your focus to engage them.

I've mentioned it before and will say it again. What often looks like a recruiting problem is frequently a RETENTION problem. It doesn't matter how fast we run the recruiting machine and get new hires in the door if we can't keep them for more than a week, 30 days, or 90 days. If that's how a piece of equipment works in a manufacturing facility, that machine will be overtaxed, stressed, and continue to break down. Steady state is your goal here, where the machine is running smoothly. Where when new hires come in, they CHOOSE to stay.

A steady state can only be achieved if you retain your team members, which you do through coaching, recognition, and engagement.

Does this mean that all turnover is bad? No, not at all.

That's part of why turnover metrics can lead to unintended negative consequences. On one hand, if we set up a goal or metric around having 0% turnover, leaders and managers are essentially being told NOT to address, coach, and even let go of poor-performing employees. On the other hand, if there are no goals or metrics around turnover, leaders and managers may not have any consequences for having high turnover on their team.

One way to keep great-performing employees engaged is by coaching, holding team members accountable, and addressing performance issues on the team. Too often, as we strive to be "nice" to others by not giving team members the feedback they NEED to hear to improve, we risk losing the engagement of our employees with the highest ROI.

ENGAGEMENT AND TRUST

According to a 2017 article in the Harvard Business Review titled "The Neuroscience of Trust,"[5] there is a direct correlation between trust and engagement. Compared with people at low-trust companies, high-trust companies report 74% less stress, 106% more energy at work, 50% higher productivity, 13% fewer sick days, **76% more engagement,** 29% more satisfaction with their lives, and 40% less burnout.

Remember a few chapters ago when we talked about trust? "Trust is built through a consistent set of behaviors repeated over time." Ken Blanchard.

Do you see the irony here? Trust is built through a consistent set of behaviors repeated over time. Have you noticed how many times we have shared this quote? *It's all about trust.*

I don't remember where I heard or learned it. As a new parent, I remember learning that babies and children watch us, their trusted adults, to see how we react and respond to different situations. This signals how they should react to things in their environment. To me, this meant that I needed to get better at staying calm during thunderstorms as my kids got older. If they saw me getting nervous and wanting to take shelter in the basement, guess what kind of response they would have? If they saw that I was responding calmly that it was normal, and that we knew what to look for and do if anything changed, then things stayed calmer for them and me.

Again, I'm not comparing our team members to children; I am simply demonstrating that human behavior at work responds very similarly. When we see our leaders losing their cool about something that "corporate" did, it becomes acceptable and permissible for us to do so, too. How we CHOOSE to react and respond has a much more significant impact when we are leaders.

---

5   *https://hbr.org/2017/01/the-neuroscience-of-trust*

THE 8 FACTORS OF ENGAGEMENT

We introduced the concept of engagement at the beginning of the book, quoting a study conducted by Buckingham and Goodall in their book, *Nine Lies About Work*. In analyzing engagement survey results, Buckingham and Goodall found that eight factors were disproportionality present in highly engaged teams.

- I am enthusiastic about the mission of my company.
- I am surrounded by people who share my values.
- My teammates have my back.
- I am confident in my company's future.
- I clearly understand what is expected of me.
- I get to use my strengths every day at work.
- I know I will be recognized for my excellent work.
- In my job, I am challenged to grow.

If we want engaged employees (which we do), we want our managers and employees to respond affirmatively to these statements. I am enthusiastic about the mission of my company. YES! I am confident in my company's future. OF COURSE! I clearly understand what is expected of me. NO DOUBT!

These eight factors are disproportionately present. I want my employees to respond affirmatively to those statements. I get it. Now what?

First, let's talk about what's NOT on this list of factors.

When we talk to our clients, business owners, and business leaders, the focus tends to be on money. Do we need to pay more? What other benefits do we need to offer? How can we compete with other businesses? How can I afford to do this?

Notice that none of these framework factors mention pay, benefits, or perks. Interesting, right? That does NOT mean that pay and benefits are not significant. However, it does mean they may not be the most important things.

YES, WE ARE TALKING ABOUT MASLOW'S HIERARCHY OF NEEDS

Do you remember learning about Maslow's hierarchy of needs in psychology classes, in high school or college? I probably put it directly in the category of "interesting things I learned that I will never use again," and yet, here we are. Maslow's hierarchy is a theory of human motivation that discusses the various levels of needs humans have.

The triangle's widest portion (the bottom two layers) are the physiological and safety needs. So, think about eating, breathing, and sleeping for physiological needs. For safety and security, think of resources, like a place to live, employment with reliable income, and health insurance. Unless we satisfy the needs at this level, our ability to meet the needs at higher levels is impossible. Having a good-paying job isn't the only thing; getting employees to engage at higher levels will require more than pay.

The middle section belongs to relationships and family. This represents the team and the community for your employees. Do your team members have relationships at work where they feel that sense of belonging? Do they have friends at work, people they (generally) get along with and enjoy working with?

The upper two sections are esteem and self-actualization. Esteem is confidence and respect, and self-actualization includes problem-solving creativity. It's bringing one's whole self to work. Do your team members see the connection to how their work makes a difference (in themselves, their teams, the business, and society)?

Our engaged employees are the employees in the top sections. Engaged employees are bringing their motivation, creativity, initiative, and problem-solving. We need to get there. What's important to understand is that we can't get to those top sections without having a foundation of safety and security with pay and benefits. Once safety and security concerns are met, though, additional income and benefits do not necessarily move someone to the level of self-actualization on their own.

What can we do to create an environment where our team members feel belonging, esteem, and self-actualization? The fun part here is that if we revisit the eight engagement factors, we start to see some connections.

Let's refocus on the eight key factors of engagement, starting with the WE experience and specific ideas and actions you can take in each area to create this environment for your team members.

We'll address the first two together:

- I am enthusiastic about the mission of my company.
- I am confident in my company's future.

Do you remember the statistics we shared earlier? Forty-four percent (44%) of employees don't know how the work they do every day impacts the business or business goals. There are a few takeaways from this.

First, this 44% is representative of all employees, including individual contributors, first-level supervisors, managers, and business leaders. We have found that the deeper the employee is in the business, the less likely they will see the connection between their work and the business goals. This percentage would likely be lower if the study only looked at business leaders and higher if the study only looked at individual contributor employees.

Second, we find that many business owners and leaders assume that employees see the connection between their work and business outcomes. Business owners and leaders believe that since *they* know how their work and their employees' work connects to the company goals, all employees know this.

Part of engaging is helping them understand the big picture and how they fit into it. What are the goals of the business – short-term and long-term? What activities help make the business successful? What impact do I, as an employee, make on achieving the business's goals? The focus is often on the work "I do this" rather than "this is WHY I do this."

I remember a story from early in my career. I was working with an external consultant who performed job audits in businesses. In a job audit, he would interview employees and ask them what they did and what their job entailed. In one company, he spoke with two individuals doing the same job. They conducted quality checks in a manufacturing environment. One person worked the day shift,and one worked the night shift. My colleague asked the day shift employee what his job was. The employee responded, "I check the parts to ensure they pass quality inspections. As the parts come down the conveyor belt, I check these items. If the parts pass inspection, I place them here, and if the parts don't pass inspection, I place them here." Okay. Sounds good. This employee knew their job. Then my colleague asked the night shift employee what her job was. This employee responded with, "MY JOB IS SAVING BABIES' LIVES! I do that by checking all the parts as they come down the conveyor belt. I check to make sure the parts pass inspection. If they do, I place them here, and if they don't pass, I place them here. But I am saving babies' lives!".

Wow. I still get goosebumps from that story. This company was responsible for making parts for incubators in the NICU.

So, which employee do you think was more engaged? The day shift employee or the night shift employee? I mean, in this case, it's pretty obvious. It's the woman who saw her role as saving babies' lives.

Now, your business is probably not manufacturing parts for incubators in the NICU, but I am guessing you have pretty cool products and stories. How can you help your employees see they are part of something extraordinary?

WHAT'S YOUR "PART OF SOMETHING BIGGER?"

A few years back, we conducted leadership training for managers and supervisors for a client who makes sealants and parts that go into construction materials for windows and doors. As part of the training, we discussed this aspect of engagement. I shared that I worked for a manufacturing business that made parts for John Deere, Polaris, and other products very early in my career. As I worked there, I constantly pointed out to my family and friends the products we made when I saw them in the 'real world.' I was so excited seeing what I made, seeing what I worked on being used daily. It was a great feeling. I asked this group of leaders and managers how they could create that same excitement about their business for their teams.

Interestingly, the group started to share cool facts about their <u>previous</u> companies. I could see excitement and engagement increase as the discussion continued. Still, I was surprised that they could share that excitement about their previous companies, especially when they were in training to do the same thing for THIS company. Finally, one individual said, "Well, did you know our products are in more than 90% of the homes in the U.S.?" Everyone in the room stopped. *What?* They didn't know that. Then a manager shared another interesting fact, and another shared a different one. The icing on the cake was when someone said, "Well, you know our products are in the Pentagon, right?" No, they didn't. The energy in the room shifted completely. It was fascinating to watch and experience.

It didn't stop there. When we returned to training the next day, a manager shared that one of his employees had told him about having products in the Pentagon. The news had spread: one manager in training told a team member, who told another one, who told another one, and someone ended up telling their manager. In less than 24 hours, this energy spread throughout the plant. *That's* powerful. That creates engagement.

Sometimes employees (and managers) just don't know those remarkable stories, and we need to find a way to share them. Sometimes we just need to provide an outlet for them to talk about it--where the discussions build on each other, and excitement continues. We need to create the space for it to happen.

Another aspect to consider is that employees (and managers) may not understand how the business runs. They don't know how the business makes money, where the money goes, what activities really drive the business's success, and what they can do to influence it.

We worked with another client who was concerned about the margin in her business (I am guessing we all have that concern). This business's main concern was shrink (scrap, waste, damage, etc.). Their leader shared a few examples with us: they were losing money by deeply discounting products and having to throw away damaged products. She couldn't figure out how to get her employees to make better decisions.

She found that she needed to start with communication, so she turned it around. The key was communication. She shared more information than she had before, and she shared the shrink amount for each location and the business overall. Before that, the employees only saw the impact of $1 or $2 here and there. They didn't see the big picture, and they didn't see how much it all added up. The key was communication. By sharing the goals, numbers, and details, employees began to see the difference in their decisions on the business and, more importantly, what they could do daily to impact the company positively.

In another case, a client was concerned that his employees didn't understand how the business operated. The employees saw all the money come in (from sales) but did not see what went out (the expenses) or what it took to operate the business. As a result, employees were getting frustrated. Frustrated because they thought money was going into the leaders' pockets and that they were missing out on it. They were also frustrated that needed improvements were not being made and that leadership decided not to make more significant investments in these improvements.

This business leader went through what he called the "penny exercise" with his employees. He divided his employees into a few groups and gave each group 100 pennies. Next, he had them go through an exercise. He asked them to think of that as their sales and guess how many pennies in each dollar went to different expenses. When the groups finished the exercise, they had 30-40 pennies set aside for profit. They were shocked when the business leader showed them the actual breakdown per dollar, and the profit from each dollar in sales was 3-4 pennies, not 30-40.

It's easy for business leaders to overlook this. We just recently realized the same thing. We have employees. We spent time talking with employees about the tasks and responsibilities, but we realized we hadn't spent much time talking about the WHY. Why did these tasks and responsibilities make a difference? How are the tasks and responsibilities helping the business achieve its goals? We scheduled a meeting and walked through the information. The company's history, how we got to where we are, the business's goals (current year and 2-3 years out), and our quarterly rocks (priorities)! They were so excited and so grateful for the information. It was all the stuff we talked about every day but spending 45 minutes sharing it with them increased their engagement and re-energized us as well.

Another way you can accomplish this is through business update meetings by proactively scheduling time to go through this information with your teams.

We've seen that the topics become very tactical when leaders sit down to create the agenda for business update meetings. It typically centers around what changes are coming up, covering their safety briefings and discussing policy changes. These are all extremely important topics. I am not minimizing the importance of these topics, and this is intended as a caution. Remember, the goal here is to engage your employees. You want your employees to respond affirmatively to feeling enthusiastic about the company's mission and having confidence in the future. So as you create your agenda, ask yourself if any of the information you cover will influence those statements. Have you provided any information or created an environment for your employees to be excited about the business, understand the bigger picture, or see how they can impact and influence the business? If not, what can you add, or what do you do to create that?

Let's move on to the last two WE experiences.

- In my team, I am surrounded by people who share my values.
- My teammates have my back.

One point of clarification, when we say "surrounded by people who share my values," that doesn't mean personal values; not every employee will have the same personal values as others. The shared values should be the values of the business. Those values you defined earlier in the book are the ones that create your intentional culture; those are the <u>shared</u> values.

First and foremost, as a leader, your primary responsibility is to role model the business's values. Employees need to see YOU behaving in ways that support and align with business values. YOU need to have your employees' backs.

More than being a role model, you must also ensure that other employees are as well. You need to hold your team accountable for demonstrating the values and behaviors. Conveniently we have already talked about many of the skills required to accomplish this. Not surprisingly, we are going back to coaching.

As you read this book, you identified the key behaviors in your business. You envisioned your intentional culture. You described your values through the behaviors and stories that demonstrate those values. You detailed the behaviors needed to reinforce the values and culture of the business. A few chapters ago, you identified your engaged employees, the rock stars and we had you think about what they did for you to identify them as engaged. That's what we are talking about. Those are the behaviors that need to be seen and experienced by your team members to feel they are surrounded by people who share their values.

When you see those behaviors, recognize them. Do you remember the client earlier who had values to honor and serve customers, each other, and the community? For team members to feel they are surrounded by others who share their values, they need to be recognized when they honor and serve customers and see their team members be recognized when they do. Recognizing team members uses our coaching skills and framework and can sound like this:

- **Set It Up and LISTEN:** "Hey, Lily. I noticed that you spent a lot of time talking to Mrs. James, and she walked away with a smile on her face. It makes me feel like the conversation went well. How do you see it?

- **Behavior:** When Mrs. James walked in, you greeted her immediately and used her name. You asked how you could help her, helped her to her car, and told her you looked forward to seeing her again.

- **Impact:** When you welcome a customer and assist them while they are here, it makes them want to come back and continue to support our business.

- **Tomorrow:** This is a great example of our value of honoring and serving our customers. Thank you. I appreciate you.

- **Solve Together**: What ideas do you have to encourage other team members to honor and serve our customers in this same way?"

Recognizing team members who are demonstrating your values is the first step. It's equally important to hold team members accountable if they are not.

- **Set It Up and LISTEN**: "Hey, Mitch. I noticed that you and Sam were unloading the truck together. You walked away before the truck was fully unloaded, and Sam continued to work. It makes me feel like you left Sam to finish the job so you could go home early. Help me understand what happened.

- **Behavior**: You left work before you finished unloading the truck.

- **Impact**: As a result, Sam had to stay an hour later last night than he expected to make sure inventory was in place before we opened this morning. One of our values is to honor and serve each other, and leaving before the work is done is not living up to our values. You were not honoring and serving Sam.

- **Tomorrow**: I expect that you honor and serve your team members by ensuring that you work until the work is done. If there is an emergency that requires you to leave before the work is done and it will negatively impact the team or the business, I expect that you talk to me so we can figure out how to complete the work.

- **Solve Together**: What can you do to ensure you are supporting your team members?"

This is an example of a team member NOT having another team member's back.

Frederick Backman said it best, "Culture is not what you say. It's what you allow,"

THERE'S NO "I" IN "TEAM," BUT THERE IS A "ME" IN "TEAM."

Now for the ME experiences. There are four:

- I clearly understand what is expected of me.
- I know I will be recognized for my excellent work.
- I get to use my strengths every day.
- In my job, I am challenged to grow.

Now, I know you know what I am going to say here. *Yep, it's coaching again.* It's about coaching employees, so they are clear on what you expect by sharing feedback on their behavior, impact, and expectations in the future. This is also finding those opportunities to recognize employees. We hear many managers struggle with this because it's easy to walk by. You don't think about it when employees are doing what they are supposed to – you notice it when employees aren't.

Coaching also ties into using employees' strengths and challenging employees to grow. But here's the thing. Many managers and supervisors, including me, assume that we know our employees' strengths, how they want to be challenged, and how they want to grow. The reality is that we don't. We assess based on our interactions, but we don't ask. Remember my story about our employee who did a great job, and I was so excited to find more projects like that?!? I was assuming, too. Thank goodness I remembered to ask.

This is a great place to use the coaching model. Take a moment to stop, ask, set it up, and listen. Ask follow-up questions and encourage your employee to share their perspective. Summarize what you heard them say. You have one tool that you can use already to really understand how an employee feels about their strengths and where they want to develop.

ENGAGEMENT QUESTIONS

Yes, the coaching model is great when you can talk about upcoming work or current projects. Sometimes you just need a conversation starter, a way to connect with employees intentionally. That's where engagement questions come in.

Engagement questions (as we call them) have also been called stay interview questions. They were set up as conversation guides managers can use with employees to encourage them to stay with you (not leave you). It usually entailed a list of questions for managers to ask employees. Unfortunately, it often becomes more of a process to complete (check the box) rather than an authentic conversation focused on listening and understanding. They also have been used when they sensed an employee was going to leave and was a last-ditch effort to keep them. Engagement doesn't start here in one big conversation; it begins with ongoing, regular discussions with our team members.

That's why we call them engagement questions, not stay interview questions. We tend to categorize them into four categories: likes, dislikes, development, and recognition. Here are a few examples.

LIKES:

- What does a great day at work look like?
- What do you like about your current job?
- What do you like most about working here?
- What are you most excited about doing in your current role?

DISLIKES:

- When have you been the most frustrated with your job?

- What about your job are you least excited about doing?
- If you could change one thing about your role or work, what would it be?
- What would you love to do that you cannot do in your current role?

DEVELOPMENT

- What skills have you learned since you started working here?
- What skills do you have that we haven't utilized?
- What skills would you like to develop this year?
- What are your career goals?

RECOGNITION:

- What types of recognition have you received that you feel acknowledged your accomplishment?
- What accomplishments are you most excited about in your job?

An interactive worksheet with these questions is available to download at www.peoplesparkconsulting.com/bookresources.

First, remember this is not a form, nor is it a process. The intent is not to ask questions for the sake of asking. The intent is to have good, ongoing conversations with your employees. We recommend asking a question or two at a time. Pick two you want to focus on and ask those in one conversation. Then for the next conversation, pick two more.

Next, understand that some of these questions may be difficult to answer without preparation. If you ask a question out of the blue, employees may not respond immediately. You can prepare your employee to answer these questions. Start by saying, "I want to make sure that you and I are connecting about your interests and goals, so over the next few weeks, I'll be asking you some questions. For our next meeting, start thinking about what you like most about your job and what you like least about your job."

Also, if you think the employee may question WHY you are asking these questions, this is a great place for using contrasting statements. "My intent is not to put you on the spot or pry, and my intent is to understand this better so that I can advocate for you as you grow and develop in your role."

It's amazing what you find out when you ask--and the impact you can have on your employees. We had a previous client who wanted to begin using engagement questions and decided to use them first on their HR team.

They had one employee working for them for about ten years who had been in her role for a while. She did what she was asked but wouldn't necessarily be considered engaged or a rockstar. She was *fine*. As they started to ask the questions, she shared a specific responsibility she had that she did not enjoy. It was the one thing she would change about her role if she had a choice. This wasn't surprising to the leaders, who could see it in the quality of her work on this responsibility.

The client also had a new employee in HR. She had been there for a few weeks when they asked her engagement questions. They asked, "What skill do you have that we haven't utilized?" She shared a skill that she really enjoyed that the leaders weren't aware of (it didn't come up in the interviews). Here's where the magic happens – the skills she mentioned she enjoyed and wanted to use were the same skills the other employee didn't like.

Can you see where I am going with this? The leaders made an easy change. They moved the responsibility from the long-term employee's plate and gave it to the new employee. And they took responsibilities from the new employee's plate that aligned better with the skillset of the long-term employee. They just did a simple swap. And BAM – both employees were more engaged.

The performance of the long-term employee improved for two reasons. First, her role was more aligned with her skillset, and she felt good about that. Second, the leaders had asked and, more importantly, LISTENED and took action based on her concerns. She wasn't just "fine" anymore in her role--she was engaged. That's powerful.

The new employee had already been excited and engaged at work-this was just elevated. Even more, within her first month in her role, her leaders showed they cared by asking and listening about what was important to her. Win! Win! Win! All because the leader **asked a few questions**.

When we share these questions, we commonly get pushback from leaders, especially questions about career goals; "What are your career goals?" Or "What is your ideal job?" The pushback we hear is, "I know this is not their ideal job, and I know that this isn't their career choice, and it's a job, not a career. What do I gain by asking that question? Why would I want to point out that this isn't their ideal job?"

Here's the thing. Their job may just be a job, not a career, and it may not be their ultimate career goal. But I guarantee there are skills they can learn and develop in their current role that will prepare them for the future.

We had a participant (a leader) in a training session who challenged this statement. He worked as a supervisor in a manufacturing environment (construction materials). He shared that his current job was not his ideal one or the one he wanted to do for the rest of his life. He said, "I want to be a chef, and how is this job going to help me become a chef?" Great question!

We asked him to start by thinking of the responsibilities of a chef. What types of skills and experiences would he need to have in a chef role, even if he wasn't in it today? Those could include planning menus, ordering products and ensuring appropriate inventory to meet the demands, and coaching and mentoring employees, to name a few. Do you see how he would develop those skill sets as a supervisor in a manufacturing plant? It was fascinating to watch this leader's body language change as this all started to sink into him. He was beginning to see how the work he did every day was preparing him for his ideal career.

As a leader, you have a very unique opportunity to connect these dots with your employees. Even when our employees are in roles they don't intend to be for the duration of their careers, we can still engage them and develop them for the time we have them with us.

CHAPTER 21

———

THE PROS AND CONS OF ENGAGEMENT PROCESSES

The answer is…[drumroll]…It depends. As with other processes we have discussed, putting structure in place to *support* engagement is a good thing, as long as it doesn't become a process for the sake of it, or a substitute for doing the work (in this case, the work of increasing engagement).

We worked with a client who wanted a sense of satisfaction and engagement from their employees (a trend we see in many clients). Before our work with them, they sent out a survey with a short note stating they wanted feedback from their employees. The response rate was low, which left the managers frustrated. So, to get more responses, they had a mandatory meeting, and employees had to fill out the survey before leaving the room. As expected, their response rate increased, and the overall feedback was mediocre. When we started working with them, they had not yet taken action on the items identified in the survey, hadn't shared any information with the employees, and didn't think they would do another.

As you read this, I am sure you are thinking, *no, of course, this was not a good process*. At the same time, what this business did was not unusual. It's actually quite common. As leaders, we start this process with good intent; we really want more engagement and for our employees to be happy at work. In spite of this good intent, we do things that hurt our engagement.

Using engagement surveys to get feedback can be a good thing. It's a data point. It's a moment in time. It keeps focus on engagement and provides good information. And you CAN increase engagement through the skills we discussed without a survey.

If you do choose to do a survey to solicit feedback, here are some considerations:

- **Provide Context.** As you ask for feedback, make sure employees understand WHY. *Why* are you gathering feedback? *Why* is it important? How does this tie to their work and business goals? What are you going to do with the information?

- **Tell Them What to Expect.** Share the timeline. Tell employees what information you will share with them and by when. Tell them what action you expect to take as a result of the feedback.

- **Share Results.** You don't have to share all the results. Highlight specific things you will share, such as the themes identified, what employees feel is going well, any common concerns, and what actions you plan to take.

- **Keep Them Updated.** Keep the information in front of your team. Share specific actions taken after the survey and the impact. Continue to ask for feedback on the steps you are taking.

- **Make It Voluntary.** Yes, the more responses you receive, the more information you will get. Yet if employees feel they are forced, you may get more responses, but they won't accurately reflect how the employees truly feel. They will share what they think you want to hear, not necessarily how they actually feel. If you want to increase the number of responses you receive, make it consistent with good communication and visible actions. Employees will see that you care, know your intent, and want to participate.

As with everything, it's about being intentional and thoughtful. Remember, "culture isn't what we say. It's what we allow." We choose our culture every day.

CHAPTER 22

——

WHEN YOU NEED TO TERMINATE

To this point, we've walked through what you can do to build your culture, reinforce it, and engage your team as your business is growing and evolving. When things get tough, though, is where your real culture shines through--for better or for worse.

We debated whether or not to even include this in the book. Ultimately, we decided to shine a light on no one's favorite topics, terminations, downsizing, and layoffs. Why? It's important to share how your culture, especially your authentic culture, shines through when the going gets tough.

For many reasons, sometimes team members aren't a good fit anymore. Assuming that you've put your coaching skills into practice, you may find yourself at a point where the next step for the employee is to leave your organization. Any time there's a decision that could impact the livelihood of another human being, it can be tough. You care about your team members and want the best for them, yet they still aren't meeting performance or behavior expectations. Balancing these risks feels heavy, and rightly so. Deciding to exit an employee does not mean that they are a bad person, or that you are. Deciding to exit an employee is a decision that is made in the best interest of your business and your team members, including the employee you are exiting.

When it comes to the actual meeting to exit an employee, many leaders get understandably nervous. I tend to have a racing heartbeat, my face and neck get red, and I internally feel like my voice is shaking. Because I've learned to understand my responses in these situations, I plan for them. I take deep breaths counting to 5 or 6 on each inhale and exhale to help my heart rate calm down. I also plan my talking points ahead of time so that if I feel nervous, I can go back to my script to ensure that my employee gets the information they need to hear as clearly as possible.

In my experience, leaders tend to talk way too much in a termination meeting. The truth of the matter is this: as long as we have been straightforward in our coaching to this point, very little in this meeting will be a surprise for them. Meeting with an employee to terminate is not sitting down to get more information, justify the decision, or argue. This meeting is to tell them the decision that's been made and the immediate next steps for them.

My rule of thumb is that a termination meeting (for performance or behavior - NOT a restructuring - we'll cover that later) should take no longer than ten minutes. Again, remember, I am assuming that leaders have had coaching conversations with this employee all along. The general script I recommend for leaders having a termination meeting sounds like this:

"Thank you for meeting with me today. Over the last few months, I've shared with you what expectations need to be met to satisfy this position's requirements. At this time, the decision has been made to end your employment with us, effective today.

You will be paid through the end of your shift today. Any PTO you've accrued and not used will be paid out in your final paycheck on <<DATE>>.

Regarding your benefits, your coverage will continue until <<DATE>>. After this point, you will receive information on how you can enroll in COBRA to continue the coverage if you would like *to do so.*

I'd like to collect the company-owned belongings in your possession - keys, credit cards, computer/laptop/cell phone. If there are any personal belongings at your desk/workstation that you would like, I am happy to get those for you.

I recognize this might be difficult, and I want to be respectful of that. We will box up belongings and have them sent directly to you. Can you please confirm the address we should ship this to?"

The script above might seem a little impersonal, even a little sterile, and that's okay. The objective of this meeting is to be clear and inform the employee about the decision that's been made (that their employment is ending), how their pay and benefits will be handled (and important dates), and the logistics of collecting personal and company belongings will be handled.

If we go back to our values and look at what behaviors are essential to our organization, we can still live these behaviors and values through tough situations like terminations. Being clear about what is happening *is* respectful and anticipating important questions (like pay and benefits) *shows care and service.* Deciding to terminate an employee can also be an act of integrity for your other team members to show how important the values really are in your organization.

RESTRUCTURING & DOWNSIZING

Termination meetings can almost seem easy compared to restructurings and downsizing, mainly because, unlike terminations, there typically isn't a performance issue or behavior concern at fault. Unfortunately, there are times when our business shifts quickly, and we need to reduce the number of employees we have, or we need employees in different roles (and our current team members are not qualified). In these instances, we must restructure the business or downsize.

Even when you face restructuring or downsizing, how you lead your team can be incredibly impactful. Think back to our chapter on change management and change communication. People dig into survival-based questions with any sort of change, like "do I have a job?" You likely don't know this answer in the early stages of assessing this. Rather than stretching the truth or outright lying, you can still demonstrate your values in your response. Remember, your employees watch how you respond and react to know how they should be.

As employees ask questions about what's going on, or if there will be layoffs, etc., your response could simply be:

> *"I appreciate you bringing up the question. Right now, I'm focused on how the business overcomes this current situation/hurdle and developing our plan to do so. I know this is important to you and all of our team members. Please know, as I have more information, I will share it with you as soon as I am able."*

Your intent isn't to hide information from anyone. Your intent is to share what you can when it is appropriate to do so. You can even say just that.

Deciding to restructure your organization or your team is not easy. Even so, you can lead through it by modeling your culture as you go.

> ***NOTE: We are <u>not</u> attorneys; nothing here should constitute legal advice. If you have questions about restructuring decisions and layoffs, we highly encourage you to partner with an employment attorney who can guide you through the process.*

First, understand the WHY behind your decision to restructure or layoff. What is the business need, and how will a restructure or layoff support it? This information and your clarity on it early on will help your communication later on. If the organization needs skills or qualifications that it doesn't have today, know that.

Next, be clear about the criteria you are using to decide who will stay and who will not be part of the organization in the future. Was this based on performance measures? Skills? If you've been following us this far, you've been coaching your team members and giving them feedback along the way about their performance. All this work helps you **and** them.

Once you've determined who may be impacted by this change, it's time to check on this for any potential adverse impact risk. This is the look of all affected employees to see if you are at risk for impacting protected groups more than others. For instance, let's say you have a team of 25 people and reduce the team by five. As you work through what you need in the business, let's say you notice that four of the five employees on your layoff list are females over the age of 40. Suppose that also happens to be a large proportion of your female workforce. In that case, you'll need to be very clear about the business reasons that these particular roles are impacted and why others weren't (strong suggestion/hint: this type of situation is *exactly* when you should engage an employment attorney).

COMMUNICATING CONSISTENT WITH YOUR VALUES

When you've reviewed your process with your employment attorney and are ready to move forward with communicating the decisions, there are some tips and practices that can make the process smoother for you and your entire team. This doesn't eliminate the stress of the situation. It does give you a framework to follow.

Remember from our discussion about change management - our goal at the beginning of this communication process is to let our employees know what will happen so they can understand the process. This also enables us to clarify our expectations for how everyone behaves during the process.

Step 1: Let everyone know what's happening.

Step 2: Meet with impacted employees individually.

Step 3: Meet with remaining employees (individually, if possible).

Step 4: Meet as a team to discuss moving forward.

STEP 1

LET EVERYONE KNOW WHAT'S HAPPENING.

Not only does this let them know what you expect from them. You can share what is happening in the business and that the business will be reducing the team to meet these current business changes. You can also share the plan to let everyone know; and that each person will meet with you individually (or with their leader). This is the point where coming back to your values can be *really* helpful:

"Out of respect for each one of you and for anyone impacted, I expect that each of us remains respectful and supportive of one another. You may find out information before others, and vice versa. Be respectful, and understand that everyone wants to know, and everyone will know."

STEP 2

MEET WITH IMPACTED EMPLOYEES INDIVIDUALLY.

I won't even try to sugarcoat this part. This sucks and can feel awful for you and your employee. Remember this: THIS IS NOT ABOUT YOU. **THIS IS ABOUT YOUR EMPLOYEE.** You can be respectful and empathetic and honor them by giving them a clear understanding of what is happening and what is next.

These discussions are likely not lengthy ones, but they are long enough to share what the employee needs to know right now. Out of respect for them, BE PREPARED.

I advise preparing an overview document for these meetings and sharing it with your employee. This overview sheet should include key information, dates, and other details we'll cover shortly. You can use this to keep your talking points on track. You can also give this document to the employee, so they have a reference sheet later on. Knowing what you're going to say and what is most important for the employee to hear is worth having your talking points ready.

Some questions you'll want to have clear answers to ahead of time include:

- When will this be effective? Does the employee need to be in the office until the effective date?

- Is there severance? How much? How is it calculated? Is there a minimum?

- What about benefits? How long will benefits last? What happens when they are no longer effective?

- Is there outplacement available? Other resources to help with a career transition?

- Is the employee eligible to apply for other roles in the company?

- When will this be communicated to other employees? Outside the company?

Years ago, in my first manager role, I had to communicate a downsizing with employees within my first month in my new role. I barely knew peoples' names and had worked through the process of determining the layoff impact with the leadership team. During this same time, I was trying to learn more about the manufacturing plant I was in, meeting employees, and learning about them and their families. While I was starting to put faces and first names together, I wasn't putting first and last names together as easily. All in all, I was getting to know first names and faces.

In our meetings to notify the impacted employees, we pulled a small group together to share information on what was happening. I knew the list on paper, but seeing those faces in the room made me feel physically sick. There were several employees I was getting to know better, and I knew details about some: one had told me about a fishing trip they took with their grandson last weekend, another had told me about their upcoming holiday plans. I learned about them, more than just the name on the paper. That's when it got real. And tough. Somehow, I remained stoic during the meetings and tried to share the information as specifically as possible. I answered questions about what it all meant. I managed to keep a calm face while still being empathetic. That was all I wanted to do during that meeting.

Afterward, though? I went straight to my office, closed the door, turned around so no one could see me, and cried. Even though I trusted that each person would be okay in the long run, I still knew that these decisions were causing pain and hurt to them right then. That felt awful. What I've come to learn is that it's okay to feel that way. I share this with you to let you know that it's normal, and that you can still lead others through with dignity and honor, even in a bad situation like that.

When you meet with your employee, you may consider using a script similar to this:

> *"Thank you for meeting with me today. As you know, we are working through some significant challenges in the business today and are restructuring/downsizing the business/department/team. As a result of this restructuring, your position is being eliminated.*
>
> *I want to share some details here about what's next and provide you with information to help answer your questions after the meeting today.*
>
> *Your last day will be XX. If you feel more comfortable, you are not required to return to the office between now and then as you transition out [only say this if it's true]. Your benefits will continue until XX, at which point you will be eligible to enroll in COBRA.*

We have developed a severance package for you. This looks like this... (go through calculations, such as one week per year of service, with a minimum of 2 weeks' pay).

I want to be respectful of you and your space as we move through the process. We will be meeting with the larger team XX to share that the restructuring communications have occurred."

STEP 3

MEET WITH REMAINING EMPLOYEES (IDEALLY, INDIVIDUALLY)

Once you've met with your impacted employees, you'll want to be sure you meet with the rest of your team. Your purpose here is to let them know their status and help them see the next step forward. You may use a script here, too, sounding like:

"I wanted to meet with you today to talk about the restructuring we're going through. Your role has not been impacted. Our business is challenged, and we have had to make some very difficult decisions that will impact team members. I feel confident that making these decisions now and moving forward with X, Y, Z initiatives will help our business get on the track it needs to be.

I value you and your contributions to our organization. Your skills in X, Y, Z and your experience in this space will be a crucial part of our success moving forward. I recognize that even though the restructuring hasn't impacted your role, it still may impact you. What questions can I help answer for you?"

STEP 4

MEET WITH THE TEAM AS A TEAM

Soon after all employees - impacted or not - have been notified, it's time to get your team back together. It likely will feel heavier than previous team meetings because it all starts to feel real that your team doesn't look like it did just yesterday.

Remember the Kübler-Ross stages of change? Your team is likely in the shock and/or denial phases right now. It's okay to let them process the change. It's also up to you to set the tone and direction to begin moving forward. Your friend during all of this? The handy questions we covered in the commitment curve.

You'll want to talk about the WHY, even though it probably feels like you've already talked about it 84,584 times. Do it again. This is your anchor, the reason the changes were made, and most importantly, talking about the risk of NOT taking action. In addition to the change related to General Understanding, you'll want to start laying the groundwork for what the team members can expect going forward. To the extent you know how some of the team's priorities are changing, share this. Lay out the steps ahead and help them see what success looks like in this new team.

Remember, these changes may have left some of your team members feeling vulnerable. The feelings of survivor's guilt (employees feeling guilty that they kept their job and their co-worker or friend didn't) are real and can be scary for your team members to work through. It's not always easy to talk about our feelings and how things make us feel, especially in a work or professional environment.

A few teams I've worked on have undergone pretty dramatic changes - restructurings, layoffs, downsizing. One of my go-to questions to get an idea of where the individual team members were emotionally was to not ask much about feelings. Instead, I ask, "What song (lyric or title) describes how you're feeling right now?" and let the team think and share. What's fascinating is how much richer the responses are than asking someone, "how are you feeling about the change?" I had answers ranging from "Don't Worry, Be Happy" to "Comfortably Numb" to "Welcome to the Jungle" to "Highway to Hell." Sure, I hadn't expected their answers to be more joking in nature, but the way I have seen teams open up with this question has provided more insights than other questions I could ask. I encourage you to consider using it in situations like this. Not only will it help get your team talking, but you can use it to assess where your team members are on their Kübler-Ross change curve as well.

Remember, your culture shows through in the tough stuff. Take the time to ensure that the values and culture you want to see in your organization are leading through them.

We mentioned earlier that books typically start at the beginning, building your team. In our experience, businesses already have a team in place when the leaders start thinking about culture, goals, and engaging and retaining their teams. We started this book where we anticipated you as a leader would be. Now, let's dig into how you continue to build your team and leverage the work you have already done up to this point.

SECTION

4

BUILD YOUR TEAM WITH SPARKS

CHAPTER 23

———

RECRUITING

Most of the time, we see organizations decide that they want to expand and create some new positions or need to replace a team member who left. We determine what the role will be and shift our attention now to the gap in their staffing to get the position filled as quickly as possible. Your intent starts out well. After all, you want to get more resources to take up some of the burden from other team members, so they don't burn out!

As the process moves on, your attention gets more and more focused on recruiting for the gap that you lose sight of your people--the ones you're trying to support in the first place. Our goal in this section is to share things you can do with the team you already have that will pay off doing double-duty: helping retain your great team members and strengthening your pipeline for new talent.

Years ago, I worked in a company in a very rural location. It was tough to recruit to the site simply because there weren't many people within a 40-mile radius. Our engineering and maintenance leader was transferred, and we opened a search for a replacement. In the meantime, we made the strange-sounding (to corporate, at least) decision to have our finance leader take on the interim coverage for the engineering and maintenance teams. It was a head-scratcher to people outside our location, but we felt it was a good fit in the meantime. Employees knew and respected them, and while engineering and maintenance wasn't their specialty, they were a strong leader.

Over the next several months, our search continued. We interviewed candidates for the role, and then as we got closer to a hiring decision, they would back out because of the location. When the plant leader and I talked, we started asking why we couldn't simply keep our setup the way it was and use the headcount in a way that would support the teams differently. We asked the interim leader, and they were willing to consider it. So, we decided to ask the team. One morning we pulled the engineering and maintenance teams together. I explained that our search was continuing, and we didn't have an update on when we expected the role to be filled. By this point, it had been months since we posted the position. Then I shared what we had been considering and that I wanted their feedback.

"We want you to think about another option. What if our interim leader stayed on as the leader full-time? We see how well the teams are working together, and in doing this, we could reallocate the headcount to a different resource, something you've said you wanted in the past. Perhaps an additional systems or controls engineer. What do you think?"

Given the technical nature of the audience, I expected them to take some time to process the questions and was shocked when they began sharing their thoughts as quickly as they did. In the few months the interim leader was in the role, the engineering and maintenance teams felt they were receiving great support and encouragement. They understood and appreciated that the interim leader didn't have the technical expertise and experience. This meant that the leader could lead in a very different way, which allowed the team members to own their roles. They quickly jumped on board and supported the idea.

That particular example has lived with me for years and is one experience I've appreciated. Leaders don't need to be technical experts in their field. Great leaders are the ones who put their faith and support into their team members to bring out their very best. Our interim leader demonstrated that to our team. It also highlights how critical it is to keep attention on your team, even as you are building it. What does your team need from you most right now? What doesn't your team need? What are they saying? What aren't they saying? Often the solutions might be with us already, but we have to pay attention to their clues.

How does this come back to what I call Inside-Out Recruiting? When we keep the attention on our team members, we're better able to see what they need. This helps us get clearer in recruiting, the selection process, onboarding new hires, and setting them up for success.

Thinking about creating a new role?

Deciding to bring on new team members is not one to take lightly. We've gone through the experience ourselves and the constant juggling of juxtaposed thoughts: *Can we afford this?* And *We can't grow without more help.* Even for organizations with well-established teams, taking on additional headcount can trigger similar thoughts and responses. As an HR professional who's had to make the tough decisions to reduce workforces based on business demand, I will appreciate those who step carefully into expansion and fully understand the personal impacts when retractions occur.

The decision to grow your team can be pretty straightforward. You see opportunities and tasks within your business that can't physically be done by you or your current team any longer. There is the temptation to jump in here and have a team member run alongside you to take these tasks on. This is where I ask you to pump the brakes for just a moment.

Before you do anything, get clear on the role and its responsibilities. I'm not talking about the title at this point. I'm talking about getting crystal clear on the primary duties and responsibilities of the person in this position. If you already have someone in mind, do your best to set that thought aside for right now. This is your business, and you need to look first at what the business needs.

Answer these two questions:

1. What does success look like for someone in this role?
2. What has to be true for you to say someone is successful in this position?

The two questions are similar and have the end in mind from the start. We want to be sure we know what success looks like to explain this to candidates. When recruiting for the position, we need to be as clear as possible with candidates about what the role entails so we energize potentially great-fitting candidates and that ill-suited candidates will select themselves out of the process. Not only does it help with recruiting, but this clarity at the beginning influences what you need for solid onboarding and sets up how you'll assess the person's performance in this role.

Remember when we shared that 44% of American workers don't know how the work, they do every day impacts the business? We can start sharing this message as early as our recruiting process to help ensure that our candidates and new hires know exactly how their role and work impact the business, for better or worse.

We've started a brief worksheet that you can use to start thinking about your next few roles. What are the primary responsibilities and tasks of the position? What does success look like? What has to be true for someone to be successful in the role? Take the time now to work through this. It will only save you time in recruiting and managing performance later.

Position	Main Responsibilities and Tasks	What does success look like?	What has to be true for someone to be successful in the role?
Administrative Assistant / Virtual Assistant	Calendar Responding to inbound questions from program participants Booking travel	The calendar is optimized (no external meetings M/F), and no-shows are reduced. 75%+ of inbound questions are fully answered by AA/VA Travel is seamless	AA/VA anticipates upcoming days and weeks with the calendar. Inbound questions are answered within 24 hours, and 75%+ are fully resolved. Repeated questions are tracked for upgrades/ education purposes and marketing.

Notice that we haven't talked about whether this team member would be a contractor, a full-time employee, or a part-time one. We must first understand the scope of what needs to be accomplished in a role before we can go to the next step, determining *how* we fill the position.

We can get creative here, and often there are several ways you can approach getting the support and skills you need in your business as it grows.

This is where I need to pause and clarify again we are NOT attorneys, and nothing that we share here is intended to be construed as legal advice.

If you have detailed questions about any of these topics, we encourage you to take the work you've already done through this book and make an appointment with an employment attorney to discuss these.

If you know what you need from the role and what success looks like, you can start to consider what type of role you have. We've seen several businesses decide to bring on an independent contractor to meet these needs. In some cases, the company doesn't need the role at a full-time level right away, as the scope is still being determined. There are ways to have independent contractors support your business that make sense for you, as long as you understand the associated risks.

Knowing whether the contractor has other businesses they support (that you aren't their only source of income) is a start, as is having a very well-defined scope of work and level of decision-making defined for the independent contractor.

Here's where the risk comes in: Often, businesses want to avoid bringing on headcount and instead opt to bring on independent contractors. On the surface, it may not scream "risky," but the rub is in how these roles are defined, the amount of decision-making involved, the level of information they are privy to, etc. If these team members are brought on as independent contractors, the business isn't obligated to pay their payroll withholding; the contractor is required to pay their own taxes. Since the team member is a contractor, not an employee, the business isn't obligated to offer them normal employee benefits.

Over the last several years, there have been large class action lawsuits regarding this exact thing - at what point is a person truly a contractor, and at what point are they indeed an employee (and should be treated as such)? To help clarify this a bit more, be sure to stay current with the IRS' 20-point checklist that asks questions about the scope and responsibility of the contractor to help you determine whether they are, in fact, a contractor or if they should be considered an employee.

Remember that this topic alone is a great reason to establish an employment attorney relationship!

THERE ARE MORE OPTIONS

There are plenty of other options, too, when you're looking to expand your team. Contractors may be one. Another might be hiring an intern, co-op, part-time employee, or consultant. Doing the work upfront to determine the role will help you choose the best route.

PROCEED WITH CAUTION!

A word of caution as you prepare to expand your team. We've seen this, unfortunately, play out with clients before: Hire for the position, *not* for a person. Just because you know someone from a previous role, or just because you had a successful working relationship before, does NOT always mean it will translate into your current business or need. The environment, the context, and the rules are all different now, and all of these can impact that relationship.

We had a client experience precisely this situation. This client was a start-up and rapidly growing, without structure or process. They brought on a team member who had previously worked within a large company and knew how to manage processes. What this new hire didn't have, and wasn't comfortable with, was the complete lack of structure (because, of course, it was a rapidly growing start-up) and the constant feeling of "flying by the seat of our pants." It strained and damaged the relationship between the two leaders, and the new hire eventually chose to go back to a larger company with a more structured environment.

Consider this cautionary tale before you send that text to your former colleague.

You can use a version of the worksheet following to think through the key responsibilities and structure for your new role. Use this alongside some other tools available (like the IRS checklist) to determine how best to structure it. We've started one below to give you an idea of some of the information we recommend getting.

Position	Key Responsibilities	W2/Employee?	Contractor? *Review the IRS Checklist*
Virtual Assistant	Complete back-end enrollment of programs Send out regular newsletters		Yes - We hire for a block of hours and are billed against them. VA has multiple other clients VA has limited access to business information
Coordinator	Central hub for client projects Share info across consultants to streamline project work	Yes. Part-time to begin. Access to company information and client info. Regular, predictable working schedule.	

RECRUITING - WHERE TO START?

Now that you've identified the role and the skills you need for your business, it's time to start recruiting! We just post a job, and people magically find us, right?

While that is how many businesses operate their recruiting, without getting the results they want and need. They fail to see all the parallels between recruiting candidates and marketing their products and services. First, just because you have a great product (or open position) and put it out there doesn't mean you are opening the floodgates. You need to build interest, educate others about your company and position, and be intentional in the process you take a candidate through, from their application to their first day with your company.

If it sounds overwhelming and a bit "much" for what you have today, hang with me. Just because you're setting up a process doesn't mean it must be complicated. Your intent should be to develop the process so that as your business grows, the process continues to scale along with you.

So what is the goal of a recruiting process in the first place? Of course, one goal is to find great talent for your position. Another important reason is to get as much information as possible throughout the recruiting process with a candidate so that you AND the candidate can make a confident decision to move forward or not. It may sound strange, but we want candidates who will *not* be great employees to self-select out of the process earlier. This reduces the amount of time and money we spend either making bad hiring decisions or having to constantly manage the performance of someone who wasn't going to be a good fit from the beginning.

Do you know the average cost of just one bad hire in an organization?

According to a 2017 study by CareerBuilder[6], across all industries, across all jobs, the AVERAGE cost of <u>one</u> bad hire was $14,900. That's PER bad hire. Sure, you can debate that some bad hires don't cost that much (you're right), and you can also debate that some bad hires cost way more than that (you're right there, too). We asked a new client how many bad hires they had made in a six-month period. Their answer? Five. Five bad hires in six months. That's $75,000, and that adds up quickly. I don't know about you, but I don't like the sound of $14,900 heading out of my business's bottom line because I didn't have enough good information on a candidate to make a strong hiring decision.

Now that I've got your attention, let's talk about some of the basic steps in the recruiting process.

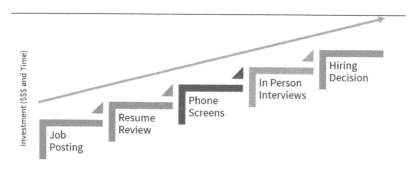

As our process moves from posting to phone screens and interviews, we invest more of our money and time into it. Our goal is to screen out candidates who will not be strong hires by getting the right information as early as possible.

JOB POSTINGS ARE NOT JOB DESCRIPTIONS

We mentioned earlier to view your recruiting process like your marketing process. It's time to get your marketing hat on. Even better,

---

6   *https://www.google.com/url?q=https://www.bizjournals.com/bizwomen/ news/latest-news/2017/12/a-bad-hire-will-cost-you-more-than-money. html?page%3Dall&sa=D&source=docs&ust=1695352434048955&us- g=AOvVaw0hf-zpp2rXIoow8fS2iIkt*

if you have a marketing resource, let's pull them into this part of the process. Suppose you did a quick search on Indeed or Glassdoor. You'd find many examples of businesses who simply cut and pasted the generic, templated, bland information directly from their job descriptions into their job postings.

This is not to say that job descriptions are not valuable. It is to say that they are a tool that can help your job posting.

When you read through those examples, does anything stand out? Probably not. If you're lucky, you might find a few extra lines about the business's history and how "fun" the team is.

If we think about it like a marketer. The job posting's Call to Action (CTA) is to get candidates to apply. That's it. That's our entire goal for the job posting. To do this, we need some of the information from the job description (so a candidate knows what the role entails). We need to tell the story of our business better, why this role is vital to it, and ensure our posting speaks directly to the candidate who would be perfect for the position.

I'm not saying to paint an always-sunny, rainbow and unicorn version of your role. We each have parts of our roles we need to do, not because we love to. I am saying to make sure your job posting speaks directly to your ideal candidate, using some of the information and words directly from your most valuable team members.

If your posting has something about a "fun workplace," let's start there. What do you hear from your employees? What do they enjoy the most? Why? How can you use your marketing hat and speak more clearly and directly to the posting?

That "fun workplace" may instead sound like "A team that enjoys working with one another, at least 95% of the time. We step in and help one another out when needed, and we aren't afraid to ask other team members for help. We trust that each one of us is doing our best that day, and we have each other's backs." See how different that

209

sounds? Our aim here is to personalize and better personify these roles for candidates. Not only does it help your posting stand out from others, but it gives better info to candidates, so the ones most fitting are more likely to apply, and the ones who wouldn't fit well aren't.

Words / Phrases in Current Job Postings	Ideas and Phrases to Re-Word Job Postings
Fun workplace	Team enjoys working with one another at least 95% of the time.
	We step in and help one another out.
	We aren't afraid to ask someone for help.
	We trust that we're all doing our best that day.
	We have each other's backs.

RESUME/APPLICATION REVIEW

Now that you've adjusted your posting and you're starting to see applications and resumes coming in, you're ready to start the review process. Because you've taken the time to review the job description and defined what success looks like for this role, you'll begin to implement this as you review candidates.

This goes without saying, but I'm going to say it anyway. At all points in the recruiting process, use CONSISTENT CRITERIA when evaluating every candidate. This means that the criteria you use to determine a strong candidate are the same for the next candidate. We'll dig more into this specifically in the interviewing process.

What should you be looking for in the resume review?

- **Experiences that relate to your role.** This may not be the easiest thing to see (especially if your candidate has been in different industries). Still, you'll want to look at the kind of work, responsibilities, and experiences they have had in previous roles.

- **Gaps in resume.** This is <u>NOT</u> to say that these are disqualifications. You can make a note of any gaps you see in the resume. Keep looking at the experiences they've had listed. If they are a candidate you want to learn more about, then we'll ask about the gaps. I make a note of the questions I want to ask, and if a candidate has some of the experiences I need, I make sure I move them onto a phone screen for more information.

Depending on the level of the role, I have other expectations for resume review. For instance, I expect candidates for leadership level roles (supervisor and above) to have solid resumes that are easy to read without typos or spelling errors. This doesn't mean that resumes with the occasional typo get weeded out. This means that I have higher expectations for these types of roles, especially since strong written and verbal communication skills *are required for success.*

As you look through the candidate's experiences, make a note (not on their resume) of their experiences that you want to learn more about. These will all help you prepare for, and get the most out of, your phone screen and in-person interviews with the candidate.

You may find a few candidates while reviewing resumes and applications that you want to meet with immediately. That's wonderful! Even if this candidate looks amazing on paper, remember that we do phone screens **and** in-person interviews to get as much information as possible to make a good decision. We intend to minimize the risk of spending $15,000 every time we make a bad hire. Sometimes when a candidate looks great on paper, and

211

we're ready to move forward with them right away, we put blinders on that prevent us from assessing the candidate's experience with the same lens we evaluate other candidates.

CHAPTER 24

INTERVIEWING

PHONE SCREENS - DO THEM!

You've seen the same memes, the ones with people looking upset, bored, or a combination, with the caption reading, "this could have been an email." Hilarious because it can be true, right?

Now I want you to think about the in-person interviews you've had with candidates. You went out of your way to schedule the time, coordinate when they would be there, who they would meet with, and questions prepared. You let the candidate know it would take about an hour or more. When the candidate arrives, and the interview begins, you find that the candidate is ill-prepared. The experiences on their resume aren't lining up the way you expected they would with your job expectations. This candidate is not going to work out. But you're only 10 minutes into this 60+ minute interview. Now you either find yourself asking a few more questions, rushing them through the questions to get finished, or saying, "Wow! Looks like we finished a little early!" at the end of the interview. Or, as tactfully as you can, share with the candidate that their experiences don't align with what you're looking for and that you will be ending the interview early. Either way is awkward and uncomfortable, especially for you as the interviewer.

This situation only needs to happen to you a couple of times before you do what you can to prevent it from happening. It's happened to me as well, which is why I wholeheartedly recommend doing phone screens for all of your candidates. This doesn't have to be video based; it can be an "old school" phone call.

Again, you're evaluating each candidate with the same criteria and asking the same questions of each candidate. These phone screens might only take 15 minutes, but you'll gain information that will make it much easier to determine what candidates you want to bring in for longer, in-person interviews. Your phone screen questions need not be complicated, either. We like to ask a couple of questions to have the candidate share more about their experience and interest in the job and one or two questions about important values or behaviors critical to this role's success. Leave room for their questions to help you understand and evaluate their level of interest in your position. In this example, a candidate must work well with others (teamwork) and quickly resolve issues (integrity).

It could be as simple as:

- Tell me about your experience as it relates to this position.
- Tell me about your interest in this job.
- One of our values is teamwork. Tell me about a time you had to work with someone you didn't like. What was the situation? What actions did you take? What happened as a result?
- Another important characteristic of our team is that we bring forward issues quickly. Tell me about a time you made a mistake and had to bring it forward to your manager. What was the situation? What actions did you take? What happened as a result?

Four questions. If you haven't conducted phone screens before for your candidates, you'll be surprised just how much you can learn about a candidate in such a short period.

ADDED BENEFIT? CANDIDATE EXPERIENCE.

Another benefit of conducting phone screens is that it gives you an additional touchpoint to build a good relationship with the candidate. At the end of the day, recruiting is a sales process. Having another great touchpoint with a candidate helps ensure that you have a good foundation in your relationship with this candidate should you extend an offer to them.

This phone screen time also allows you to tell the candidate what to expect from here. If you want to bring this candidate in for an interview, you can use the end of this phone screen to share that.

> "I've really enjoyed getting to know more about your experiences on our call today. Our hiring process also includes a more in-depth in-person interview, where you'll meet with me and a few team members. We'll be able to share more with you about the business and know more about your experiences as they relate to this role. From there, we evaluate all candidates and decide on how we move forward with candidates.
>
> I'd like to invite you to meet a few team members during that interview. What is your availability for about 2 hours next week? Here are the days that are available for us."

Feels pretty good, doesn't it?

I recently talked with a colleague about their own experience as a candidate for a new position. I was most curious about what he experienced in the recruiting process. What did he enjoy the most about the process? After a few seconds of thought, he shared this:

"It's nice to feel wanted."

215

BEHAVIOR-BASED INTERVIEW QUESTIONS

I don't know if you've heard this before, but in general, interviewing is not the most reliable predictor of a candidate's success in a job. Why? People can tell great stories and anticipate what you want to hear in an interview, just to get the offer. It can lead hiring managers and business leaders to wonder who in the world is showing up every day at this job (because it isn't the same person who interviewed them). I'm sure you've been there before. I know I have.

The reliability of interviewing can be improved as a predictor of a candidate's success in a job through behavior-based interviewing. Behavior-based interviewing involves asking candidates questions and sharing actual examples of situations they've encountered before, how they handled them, and what happened as a result. Behavioral-based interview questions begin with:

- Tell me about a time when...
- Give me an example of...

Behavior-based interview questions dig into specific job responsibilities/experiences, values, and behaviors that a person has previously experienced. How someone has handled a similar situation in the past is a closer predictor of their success in the future (albeit not perfect, either).

Here's how I look at this: We all know what we SHOULD do in a given situation. I know I *shouldn't* raise my voice when an angry customer gets in my face. I know I *shouldn't* roll my eyes when I disagree with the direction someone is taking or when I have to work with someone I don't like.

Just because I know what I SHOULD do in those situations does NOT mean that it is what I have *actually* done in previous cases. That's the aim of the behavior-based interview question - to not give a hypothetical (what "*should*" you do?) question to a candidate, but rather have them share with you an example of what they DID do.

We see the eye rolls whenever we say, "Tell me about a time when…." We hear the "this is too complicated for me and my business" responses. All of these are normal, AND these are all workable.

Where do you even start? Get out that list of values and the list of key responsibilities you developed for the position. Along with the values, these are likely what you want to see consistently across your organization, so coming up with some solid behavior-based interview questions here means that you can use this same set of questions for all candidates, regardless of role. You'll tailor your job-specific questions based on the responsibilities to learn about the candidate's experience related to them. Let's start with the values-based questions.

If you're like several of our clients, you might have similar values around integrity, customer service, and teamwork. You've also gone through the work earlier to identify what these values look like at the behavior level.

For integrity, you want to see people who will bring forward and take responsibility for their mistakes. You don't want people who hide issues until they become so big that it takes time, energy, and resources to address them.

Some behavior-based interview questions related to this could sound like this:

> "*Tell me about a time you made a mistake and had to bring it forward to a manager or leader.*"
>
> "*Tell me about a time you hesitated to bring forward a mistake to a leader or manager.*"
>
> "*Tell me about a time you caught a mistake early and were*

able to resolve it."

For customer service, we might want to find a team member who can anticipate the needs of our customers. We want a team member who can calmly diffuse difficult situations with angry customers without just giving in to (all of) a customer's needs. We want a team member who can manage multiple priorities while giving great customer attention.

Some questions here could sound like this:

> *"Tell me about a time you anticipated the needs of a customer and were able to suggest items or services to them based on the relationship you built with them."*

> *"Tell me about a time you had an angry customer and had to diffuse the situation."*

> *"Tell me about a time you had several customers needing your attention at the same time."*

With teamwork, we may want to find employees willing to step in and help someone else out, not someone who waits to be told what to do. We may also want our team to work professionally with one another, even if they don't get along. Finally, we may also want our team members to have the courage to speak up among their team if they don't feel like something is right.

Your questions might sound like this:

> *"Tell me about a time you stepped in to help a team member, even if they didn't ask."*

> *"Tell me about a time when you had to work with someone you didn't get along with."*

> *"Tell me about a time you stood up to support a team member when you didn't feel something was right."*

Overall, the questions need to relate to the business's behaviors you WANT to see or DON'T want to see. They don't have to be fancy corporate talk. They simply need to sound like YOU and know what's important in your business. Get specific on those behaviors and actions and start working on "tell me about a time when..." and "give me an example when..." to get your own behavior-based questions.

What are some of the values and behaviors you want to screen for in your interviews? We've started the table below to get you started.

Value / Behavior	Behavior-Based Interview Question
Teamwork	Tell me about a time you had to work with someone you didn't get along with.
Customer Service	Tell me about a time you had an angry customer and had to de-escalate the situation.
Integrity	Tell me about a time you made a mistake at work and had to bring it forward to get it resolved.

An interaction worksheet to create interview questions is available for download at www.peoplesparkconsulting.com/bookresources. The worksheet also includes a resource with examples of questions for the most commonly used values and behaviors.

CONSISTENT QUESTIONS.

I am a huge fan of having consistent interview guides when it comes to interviewing. Not only do I hate scrambling at the last minute before an interview, but the advantages of consistent questions are also too good to pass up. You'll start to see the magic happen when you ask a core set of questions across several candidates. You will start seeing the differences between strong and weak answers and stronger candidates and weaker ones. That right there is the whole point of behavior-based interviewing; to learn enough about the candidates to decide whether or not to move forward in the process. That's it.

I've found that I can have a standard set of questions related to business-culture, values, and behaviors to use with ALL candidates, regardless of role. In addition to these questions, I craft more specific questions about the job duties and responsibilities of the role I'm recruiting.

For instance, if I'm recruiting for a supervisor-level position, I will need to be sure I have questions related to that candidate's experience managing a team. These questions are more **job-related** and can still use behavior-based interview questions.

> *Tell me about a time when you had to manage a performance issue with a member of your team.*

> *Tell me about a time you had to motivate a team to meet a really aggressive deadline.*

> *Tell me about a time you saw an opportunity to develop a team member into a more prominent role.*

Some businesses choose to have separate questions for each role, though I prefer to have guides primarily separated by the role level. This could be broken out to be something like Manager, Production, Sales, or Administrative. It could also be broken out as straightforward as Exempt, Non-Exempt, People Leader. You may start here and see what additional adjustments you need based on how your business continues to grow.

INTERVIEWING:
MORE THAN ASKING, IT'S ABOUT GETTING INFORMATION

I've seen so many instances (and earlier in my career, I have lived them myself) where managers interview candidates, ask the question, listen for the first response, and then move on to the next question without probing. In more instances than not, though, we have barely scratched the surface of the answer.

There is so much more to interviewing, and rushing through questions leaves you with candidates who might tell a great fluff story (that actually has no substance of value). It may also leave you with a candidate who's less confident and has a hard time coming up with a situation to talk about. It might seem like you can do nothing in these situations, but there is SO MUCH.

STAR

I don't know why, but HR people like using STAR as the title for lots of frameworks, models, and acronyms. I'm warning you now because the framework I will share with you is called STAR.

S = Situation

T = Task

A = Action

R = Result

I learned this (many, many) years ago in grad school when I was being taught how to answer behavioral-based interview questions as a candidate. As someone who hadn't intended on recruiting or going through this in the first place, it was all foreign to me.

STAR keeps people like me (and many candidates) focused during an interview so candidates can give an interviewer the information they need to make a good hiring decision. The intent here is to learn more about the Situation or Task, what Actions the candidate took, and the Result of those actions.

Over the years, I've found that I like STAR even more as an interviewer. STAR keeps me focused on ensuring I listen to the candidate's responses and get all the information I need from their answers. One of the best things? The STAR follow-up questions are the SAME as your behavior-based interview questions; you use the same ones every time you ask a behavior-based question. Here's how they sound:

- What was the Situation or Task?
- What Actions did you take?
- What happened as a Result?

Seriously. Same follow-up questions, every time.

STAR gives you a fill-in-the-blank so that you can capture notes around what elements of the STAR you are getting from your candidate's answer. Did the candidate forget to tell you the specific actions they took? Now you have your probing question: *"Thanks for that answer. What specific actions did you take in this example?"*

Did the candidate tell you the Situation and Actions, but the result wasn't clear? That's your question, "Thanks for your example. What happened as a result?"

You may find that you're staying on questions a little longer than you used to, and that's okay. It's (as Kristen says) "digging past the FLUFF to get to the STUFF."

Another advantage of STAR is that it can help keep an interview more conversational. You can use STAR to coach your candidate through the questions to make sure they're sharing all the information you need in their examples. You can start by asking, "Tell me about a time when you had to work with someone you didn't like. What was the Situation?"

In asking the question this way, you're taking a typically high-stress situation (like an interview) and making it more conversational - while still staying on point with your questions. As the candidate shares their answers, listen and take notes, seeing which STAR elements their answers complete. Then, when they finish, if they weren't clear on the Actions taken or the Results they achieved, your follow-up questions are much more targeted and on-script (using the

STAR questions).

For instance, if your candidate gave a decent answer, but the Actions were unclear, your follow-up to them might sound like, "Thanks for sharing that example. What were the Actions you took specifically? What was your role on that team?"

Again, you're staying on target by following STAR and giving your candidate clear information about what you are looking for in your answer. We've had managers tell us that their businesses aren't that big and they don't need to be so formal in their interviews. Remember, the point here isn't to be formal and "corporate." The point here is to get the best information possible about a candidate so you can make a good hiring decision, not a lousy one.

Using STAR as the guide for your interviews, you will likely find that you spend more time on a question with a candidate. You might also feel uncomfortable or awkward having to restate a question to get the necessary information. This is mostly because you're ensuring you have all the STAR elements. In addition, you may see a common scenario we've encountered: an interview answer that didn't start off very impressive was pretty powerful as you dug in with your STAR follow-up questions. The reverse happens, too. That candidate that seemingly, on paper, is a PERFECT fit somehow falls flat when you start digging in to ask about the specific actions they took, their role on their team, and the results.

Recently, we had a manager go through our training. He didn't buy into STAR and told us he had an interview that evening for an entry-level laborer position. Though he was reluctant, he agreed to use STAR in his interview. The following day, he shared with us that a candidate's answer about building a chicken coop (of all things) turned out to be a really good example of the value [teamwork] he was probing than it appeared on the surface. He even shared that "in the past, I would have heard the first part and moved onto the next question. I asked the follow-up questions and found more to the story that was really helpful. He was a stronger candidate than I thought." We often find more to the stories than what we hear on the surface. Without knowing WHAT to ask, we simply take in the surface story and move on from there. Imagine what you might uncover from your candidates!

PREPPING CANDIDATES

We get it. Sometimes you're in an industry or an area where it seems like there is a lot of formality in doing behavior-based interviews, and you know others just aren't doing them. While I can't speak for what other companies are doing, I can't oversell just how important having a consistent set of (behavior-based) questions is and how using STAR in every interview is critical. Of course, I was going to say that - I'm the HR person.

That said, many times, candidates aren't used to interviewing, either. Even without formal questions, the process of sharing your experiences and information with strangers, so they make an employment decision is nerve-wracking. And rightly so. I am not saying to give the candidate the interview guide to help them prepare, I am saying there are things you can do to help your candidate bring their best self to the interview. An unintended benefit? This type of "candidate experience" goes a long way, especially when other companies show their candidates an experience that is more similar to moving cattle. Not so good.

Since you've taken the time to identify your values and key organizational behaviors, use this as your guide. You can even use the words in the examples below to help communicate to candidates before you bring them in for an in-person interview.

We are excited to meet with you and learn more about your experiences on <<DATE>> at <<TIME>>. To help you prepare for your interview, I wanted to share a little more about what to expect.

> A couple of our most important values are <<VALUE>>, <<VALUE>>, and <<VALUE>>. Behaviors demonstrating this are how we are expected to work and support our customers daily.
>
> In our interview, we will ask you questions about these values and experiences you've had where these have been demonstrated. Take some time to think about examples that relate to these values and consider what questions you have for us.

What you're doing here is 1) confirming the interview details and 2) telling the candidate how they can best prepare for their interview. You're giving them an opportunity to bring their best self to the interview without giving them the questions. I can guarantee most businesses are not doing this, which is a way you can stand out. You can keep it general like this or even add a little more about your organization or what a candidate can expect in the process.

HAVE YOU UNINTENTIONALLY LOWERED YOUR STANDARDS?

> "The labor market is too tight, I can't find enough good candidates, and I don't have time to interview the candidates I do get."

Sound familiar? If so, you're not alone. There might not be many candidates for your roles, and you feel pressured that SOME-BODY is better than NO-BODY. Many of our clients operate in rural areas, and in places where the labor market is limited.

I want to challenge that for a moment because, in our focus on what we don't have at a given time, we can cause unnecessary and time-consuming issues later by unintentionally lowering our hiring standards.

If, on a scale from 1 to 10, our candidates would typically be a 7 to

10, we feel pretty good. We know what kind of talent we're bringing in, and we can keep pretty consistent expectations with our team members as they start. They know what we're about, we know what they're about, and there's a good relationship. Our current team members also trust that we're keeping them in mind as we add new employees, and our hiring decisions will help them, not hurt them.

That's all lovely, isn't it? But what happens if the candidates we're seeing now are really only a 4 or 5 on that same scale? When we rush to hire candidates, we usually wouldn't, there are several unintended consequences for you to watch for in your business.

If we don't use the same questions of these candidates, we miss the opportunity to set our expectations with them. If candidates see that all they have to do is show up (or show up at least part of the time), then we've just lowered our bar altogether.

If we lower our bar for these incoming candidates, those team members we're trying to support and clone see this clear as day, and it doesn't take long for them to wonder why *they* should work by different rules or expectations. Even worse? Our actions here are disengaging the very employees who have been engaged in our business!

You might still make an offer to a candidate who's a 4 or 5. It's important to set the same high standards and expectations for them.

CHAPTER 25

HIRING AND ONBOARDING

Yay! At this point, you've identified someone you want to bring to your team - that's exciting! Our goal is to get them on-board and productive. This usually translates to getting their paperwork filled out, giving them a tour, showing them how to punch in, and partnering them with a team member to learn the job.

Those are all important things, so let's start back at the beginning. There's more to bringing in a new team member than showing them where the break room is located. This is also about building a relationship with your new team member and trust. The investment you make in this relationship early on is what will drive engagement. Think of the activities between the point of offer and the employee's first few months at work. What could you do to build trust?

You begin to build a relationship with your new employee by connecting with them before they begin work. Call them to offer the position, call the day before they start work and share your excitement about their first day, and contact them in between to see if they have any questions.

While offer letters are seen as a way to document employment details, it's also a way to build trust by ensuring you are on the same page. It's a way to build excitement and for the new employee to feel valued because you took the time to make them feel connected and important.

Other practical activities also can make or break a new employee's first day on the job.

- Build a plan for the employee's first day and share this information with other team members.
- Schedule time with them on the first day, so they know they are important to you.
- Ensure the new employee has everything they need to do their job (there is nothing like showing up as a new employee and your leader is trying to find a place for you to sit for the day).

ORIENTATION (AND NEW HIRE PAPERWORK) DOES NOT EQUAL ONBOARDING

That's correct, and it's a misunderstanding we see regularly. Are there mandatory practices we should have in our process for new hires? Absolutely - we do not want you to violate any of your responsibilities as an employer. And onboarding goes beyond this. A recent study showed that 58% of organizations' onboarding programs were focused only on processes and paperwork.

We look at orientation as the basics. This is where we go over the new hire paperwork, of course, AND we also start to share the basics about their role and the business with our new hire.

In addition, there is onboarding. Onboarding is about engagement. This is how we're providing reliable cues that our new hires can expect throughout their employment with us - where we're explaining the business, the culture, the goals, and the expectations of team members.

In the table below, we started to outline activities that are typically included in orientation and onboarding. Now think back to the eight factors of engagement, the **Me** experiences, and the **We** experiences from earlier. Where do you see 'We' experiences show up? These are primarily in the Onboarding column, with the mission, values, behaviors, and goals—the alignment through discussion about how the new employee's work aligns with the business's success.

Orientation	Onboarding
• Introduce to coworkers. • Tour of business. • Provide employee handbook. • Review relevant policies. • Train on-time reporting. • Complete new hire paperwork. • Teach specific job responsibilities.	• Discuss company mission, vision, and values. • Provide examples and stories of behaviors that support values. • Review business goals and strategies. • Discuss how their work leads to company success (alignment). • Have regular check-in meetings.

Use this as your starting point and be sure you're getting into more detail. Remember, onboarding is more than new hire paperwork and training someone to do their job. Your new hire has already begun to experience your culture through their recruiting, interviewing, and hiring processes. Now that they're an employee, they can see whether they were sold something or whether your culture really is what you say it is.

We worked with a client to build their onboarding process. They had the orientation stuff in place, what paperwork needed to be filled out, a review of the employee handbook, and training. They had intentionally defined their culture, values, behaviors, and goals and wanted that to come to life with the new employees.

We looked at their onboarding in three ways: onboarding to the business, onboarding to the team, and onboarding to the job. They found most of their focus was onboarding to the job and the training to do the job. As they developed their onboarding process, the client put together information on the history of the business, values, behaviors, expectations, and goals to focus on onboarding to the business. The information is spread across a series of meetings (not all at once) to allow the employee time to absorb the information. This allowed them to see the values, behaviors, and expectations demonstrated in the workplace and ask questions.

When onboarding, leaders identified key individuals with whom the employee would work and ensured that time was set up with each to begin building those relationships.

Onboarding to the job includes training on the job responsibilities and assigning the new employee a buddy or mentor.

Looking at the onboarding in these three ways allowed the leaders to make the most of the onboarding of their new employees. One of their leaders shared with us some feedback from a recent new employee. The leader had asked the employee how he was feeling, and the employee said that "he had never felt so valued." YES! That's what we want!

IT ALL COMES BACK TO COACHING

Yes, of course, we will bring this back to coaching. This is where the **Me** experiences come into play. Especially as a new hire begins and is acclimating to the organization, to their team, and learning their role within it.

There's a reason we talk about change management in this book and about how people feel and work through change. It shows up in many parts of our employees' tenure with us. It isn't just about when a new project or initiative starts; it's also when we begin in new roles or take on new responsibilities. The truth is, we go through the change cycle far more than we may realize.

Starting with a new company, and beginning the onboarding process with a new hire, is an excellent example of going through the change process all over again. Remember when you went through it? You may have felt competent and good at what you did in your previous role. You had an opportunity to start with a new organization, and within the first couple of weeks, you felt the "AHHH!! I'm never going to get this?! Why did I do this?!" response that we all go through.

When you make that offer to your new hire, they're getting perched on the left side of that Kübler-Ross change curve. Your onboarding process and the coaching you provide them in those first few hours, days, and weeks WILL make a significant difference in whether they choose to stay and how quickly they can get themselves up to fully functioning.

Various studies have shown that up to a third of new hires quit their jobs in the first 90 days. Go ahead and read that line again. A third!

I don't know about you, but the thought that all the time and effort going into recruiting and interviewing candidates to have a third still leave in the first 90 days is alarming. It's easy to point to external reasons outside of your control as the culprits. You think, *It's the generation*, and *No one wants to work anymore*, or *Everyone needs to have their hands held to know what to do.* It's easy to believe that there isn't anything we can do about it.

If we can move someone through their change curve more quickly and more effectively, we give ourselves a better opportunity for them to stay with us. Those turnover numbers start to drop after 90 days pretty significantly.

Think about the environment you have created for your new hires today. Are they left on their own, expected to figure things out? Are they partnered up with a more tenured employee to teach them how to be successful in their role (a follow-up question - does the tenured employee WANT to train and teach a new hire? Sadly, we're far too familiar with instances where this good intent has gone horribly wrong for employers)? Do they know when they'll connect with their leader? Are they given the ability to ask questions, and are those questions heard and valued?

Not surprisingly, coming back to coaching can support your new hire throughout the onboarding process. My go-to with new employees is Set it Up and Listen. What a great opportunity to ask a new employee how they're doing in a way that's more productive than simply "how's it going?"

For instance, your new hire that's getting the hang of the role? Your Set it Up and Listen could sound like this:

> "I noticed that your production numbers have increased since you went through your training.
>
> It makes me feel like you understand it and are getting the hang of it.
>
> How do you see it?"

Even more critically is picking up when something just seems "off" in those first few weeks with a new hire. When you feel like you want to say something but aren't quite sure even where to start:

> "I noticed you've had your head down more and have been sitting alone more the last several days.
>
> It leads me to believe that you're not feeling

comfortable.

What are your thoughts?"

Remember, we don't always have to go step-by-step through the coaching model. In instances like these with new hires, staying curious and asking open-ended questions helps you build trust with them, but it also helps you uncover potential issues when they're still solvable. If you do nothing else, observe, be curious, and ask questions.

SECTION

5

BRINGING IT ALL TOGETHER

CHAPTER 26

IT'S PROCESS AND SKILL

We started this book focusing on how you can achieve your business results to build and sustain the culture you want. For most business owners and leaders, that translates to having HR processes. Yes, **and** we hope you see from the information we provided that it's more than that. It's about seeing the goals and what you want to achieve -- the big picture. It's about understanding the importance of having an engaged team and what actions impact team engagement. It's about having the skill to engage your team and having the processes to support the engagement. Knowing that engagement is important and having the skills to accomplish what makes the process successful.

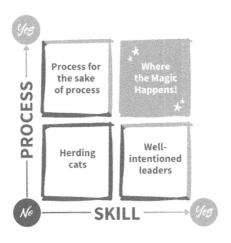

Typically when we start working with a client, their focus is on HR processes (you have heard that theme throughout the book). If you have a process without the importance and skill, it will turn into a process for the sake of the process. You and your managers will spend your time, energy, and resources on processes and forms without achieving any of the results for the business or engagement of the team. Your team members will feel they aren't valued, as if you are meeting with them to complete the process, not because you care.

On the other hand, you could have highly skilled and motivated leaders and no processes. In that case, you will have well-intentioned leaders doing what they feel is best, with each of them going a different direction because there is no road. They are using processes or tools from their previous jobs that may or may not (most likely do not) align with where you want to go. They give feedback and recognize behaviors they individually value but are not focused on the intentional culture you want for your business.

That is why we focus on both. Processes can be implemented, and other than adjusting from time to time, as goals change and new tools are introduced, they are pretty straightforward and stable. When new employees and leaders are hired, you train them on the process. Developing and implementing skills is more complex, and it's not a check-the-box activity. Building these skills and muscles takes time, work, and intention. You are creating new habits for yourself, AND your leaders need to develop these habits. When you hire new leaders (or promote leaders from within), the skills are not something that you can sit down and explain in a meeting or with a flowchart.

CHAPTER 27

NEXT STEPS

What stands out to you now that we've taken you through some of our favorite tools and concepts? If your head is spinning a bit, that's okay. It is normal to feel like you're ready to start trying out ALL of the concepts and tools and suddenly feel like you're paralyzed and unable to do any one thing. Remember that dimmer switch concept? That's what we're talking about here. You won't just wake up on Friday and magically be great at coaching, providing feedback, and leading through change. Instead, what can you do today / this morning / in the next hour that will move your dimmer switch as a leader up a smidge?

One thing that drives me bananas about management and leadership books is the "YES! I can do this!" feeling I get when reading them. Then, suddenly, that turns into feeling like I don't know where to start. Then, I begin to question whether I'm "doing it right" when I try implementing it. To help you make this transition from reading, soaking it up, and simmering on it into ACTION, we've developed a workbook for you to accompany your progress.

While it can be so much easier to throw our hands up and blame anyone (or more) of the following: the economy, inflation, the labor market, my busy-ness, my industry, etc. as the reason we don't have the culture in our business that we want, the heart of the matter

239

is that there is more in our control and circle of influence than we sometimes care to admit to ourselves.

It's right here waiting for us to notice, look at, and develop intentionally.

You have the tools to ignite the culture you want in your organization already. It's your People Spark®.

ACKNOWLEDGEMENTS

———

We have been on an incredible journey. There are so many people who have been on this journey with us. Some we have known forever, some we have just met. Some started as strangers and have become colleagues and friends. Most have impacted us in ways that we did not expect and we will forever be grateful.

Thank you to those who believed in and supported us. Sharing news like "we're starting a business" or "we're writing a book" is scary. We were overwhelmed by the responses from those around us, "that's incredible!", "you got this!", "what can I do to support you?", and "how can I help you?". We are here today because of the amazing support we received.

Thank you to the business leaders we have had the privilege of working with through the years. You welcomed us into your businesses and taught us about the agriculture industry and the incredible impact it has on every human. We are honored to have the opportunity to walk alongside you. You are not clients, you are friends, for which we are truly grateful. We appreciate you.

Thank you to the mentors and peers we have met along the way. You have been our fan club cheering us on from the sidelines lines. You have been our coaches, pushing us to be more than we thought we could be, challenging us to go further, and delivering tough messages when they needed to be delivered. You have and still do impact our lives personally and professionally in ways that we never could have imagined. Thank you.

Thank you to our team. And wow, what a team! We are so grateful for each of you. You believe in the work we do, you work hard every day for our clients, and you love our clients as much as we do. We are excited to have you on Team People Spark®. Thank you.

Thank you to our families, our husbands, and our kids. You took the biggest risk with us and beside us. You trusted us and supported us. You stood by our sides during challenging times and celebrated with us for the exciting times. We love you.